WRITERS AND CRITICS

Chief Editors
A. NORMAN JEFFARES
R. L. C. LORIMER

Advisory Editors
DAVID DAICHES   C. P. SNOW

HOPKINS

NORMAN H. MACKENZIE

OLIVER AND BOYD

EDINBURGH
LONDON

OLIVER AND BOYD LTD
Tweeddale Court
Edinburgh 1

39A Welbeck Street
London W.1

First published 1968

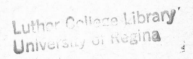
Printed in Great Britain
for Oliver and Boyd Ltd
by Robert Cunningham and Sons Ltd
Alva
Scotland

CONTENTS

ACKNOWLEDGMENTS

No perfunctory thanks could repay the kindness and encouragement which I have received from the Society of Jesus during the vicissitudes of writing this book. At Campion Hall, Oxford, the Rev. Deryck Hanshell, s.j., and the Rev. B. Fitzgibbon, s.j., made me their frequent guest while I was working on the Hopkins Ms. collection. To the editor of *The Month*, the Rev. R. Moffat, s.j., and to Mr R. Brown I owe the freest access to the library at Farm Street, London. I was also given a cordial welcome at St Beuno's College, Manresa House, Stonyhurst, and University College, Dublin; and the Rev. Alfred Thomas, s.j., passed on to me information concerning the poet's visit to Rhyl. I am most grateful to the Society of Jesus for permission to quote many unpublished versions of Hopkins's poems.

A major debt is to the Rt Hon. Lord Bridges, who has been most generous in allowing me to use original Hopkins Mss. and in giving me the benefit of his scholarly knowledge. The editors of this series, particularly Professor A. N. Jeffares and Mr R. L. C. Lorimer, deserve my sincere gratitude for their patience and humanity during the delays occasioned by the loss of the original Ms. of this book, and my subsequent preoccupation with the Fourth Edition of the *Poems*.

The texts of Hopkins's published work are included by kind permission of Oxford University Press and the Society of Jesus. We thank the Athlone Press for permission to quote from J. Sambrook: *A Poet Hidden*, and Winifred Nowottny: *The Language Poets Use*; and the Oxford University Press for the quotation from John Pick: *Gerard Manley Hopkins*.

N. H. M.

LIST OF PRINCIPAL POEMS DISCUSSED
IN CHRONOLOGICAL ORDER

ABBREVIATED TITLES BY WHICH HOPKINS'S
WORKS ARE CITED IN FOOTNOTES

Poems	=	*Poems*, 4th edn., edd. Gardner and MacKenzie.
Letters	=	*The Letters of Gerard Manley Hopkins to Robert Bridges.*
Correspondence	=	*The Correspondence of Gerard Manley Hopkins and Richard Watson Dixon.*
Further Letters	=	*Further Letters of Gerard Manley Hopkins, including his Correspondence with Coventry Patmore*, 2nd edn., 1956.
J.P.	=	*The Journals and Papers.*
S.D.W.	=	*The Sermons and Devotional Writings.*

CHAPTER I

THE SECRET POET

The funeral epigram of Aeschylus (the great Greek dramatist whose tragedies held Hopkins's admiration throughout his life) made no mention of his *Prometheus* or *The Seven against Thebes*. Giving his father's name and his birthplace, it added in simple pride: "His valour the glorious grove of Marathon did witness and the long-haired Medes learned to their cost." If Hopkins had composed his own epitaph he would probably have omitted all reference to his poetry, which in later years he had taken pains to conceal from all but a few of his closest friends. Using the Ignatian military metaphor, he might merely have written in unprophetic modesty: "Though he brought the Society of Jesus no glory, he never wavered in his allegiance." The relationship between his ascetic and aesthetic urges has given rise to much misguided speculation on the part of his critics and caused the sharpest division of opinion. In this introduction to Hopkins we can only touch upon a few of the salient features in a life which somewhat resembled that of St Alphonsus Rodriquez, which Hopkins described in his own self-revealing sonnet as one of outward placidity concealing a ceaseless spiritual warfare.[1]

Gerard Manley Hopkins might with appropriate training have made his name as an artist or a musician, for he was the most gifted member of a gifted family. When he was born (28 July 1844), his father Manley

[1] This biographical chapter has been considerably curtailed in view of the forthcoming biography of Gerard Manley Hopkins by the great authority on this subject, Fr Anthony Bischoff, s.j.

Hopkins had already published a first volume of verse, *A Philosopher's Stone and Other Poems*. Two of his brothers became artists, and one of his sisters, Grace, had an exceptional musical talent.

Most of Gerard's education was received at Sir Roger Cholmeley's Grammar School at Highgate, which was then acquiring a reputation for scholarship under Dr Dyne. W. W. Skeat, who spent three years in the school just before Hopkins entered in 1854, recalled with gratitude a then unusual feature of the school's curriculum which may have encouraged young Hopkins in the writing of verse:

> Our headmaster had one somewhat uncommon idea, which savoured, as it has always seemed to me, of great wisdom. Instead of invariably requiring us to turn English poetry into Latin verse, he sometimes gave us pieces of Latin poetry to turn into English verse; a change which was delightful and refreshing. The English verse was usually poor enough, but the attempt to produce it was stimulating and valuable. And he did more than this; for our usual holiday task, in the longest holidays, was to produce an English poem of 200 lines on a given theme.

Skeat considered that these experiments probably helped to breed from the school its one genuine poet. But his allusion was not to Hopkins (with whom he had corresponded on etymological matters). To the end of his days Skeat thought that Philip Worsley—a name scarcely known today—was the only poet of merit to whom Highgate School could point.[2]

Worsley had brought honour to his old school by winning the Newdigate Poetry Prize at Oxford in 1857, a feat which Dr Dyne must have hoped would be remembered and emulated, since he set the Newdigate subject

[2] W. W. Skeat, *A Student's Pastime*, 1896, pp. viii ff., a book overlooked as illuminating G.M.H.'s schooldays.

for his own school poetry prize in 1860—"The Escorial".
Hopkins's winning entry is the earliest of his surviving
work.[3] As one reads these rich Spenserian stanzas,
melodious parallels from "Mariana in the South" and
the "Eve of St Agnes" form a subdued counter-theme.
The influence of Keats may have been strengthened by
the presence on the staff, though only for a short half-
year, of R. W. Dixon, a poet himself, "who would praise
Keats by the hour", and with whom Hopkins later held
a rewarding correspondence.[4] Dixon remembered Hopkins as "a pale young boy, very light and active, with a
very meditative and intellectual face". A fellow student
after his death recalled him as "quiet, gentle, always
nice . . . a charming boy from a master's point of view".[5]

But Dr Dyne, like many another Victorian head-
master, believed that the best way to implant an enthusiasm for the classics in a boy was with the "rod of
forc'd persuasion".[6] His students thought of Dyne as a
man lacking in tact, judgment of character, and im-
partiality.[7] He disliked Hopkins for his independence
and championship of anyone whom he considered un-
fairly treated; and though this won Hopkins the respect
of his fellows, it led to endless conflicts with Dr Dyne.
Of Dyne's delight in flogging we have considerable evidence, and one wonders how much the "melancholia"
from which Hopkins suffered all his life was aggravated
by those schooldays. The Victorian overemphasis upon
the need for absolute and fearful obedience affected their
theology as well as their schools: if Hopkins associated
the wielding of the lashed rod with divine correction, he
had a poor earthly model of authority to remember.[8]

[3] *Poems*, pp. 3 and liv (Foreword). Previous printings are full of
errors.   [4] *Correspondence*, pp. 4-6.
[5] C. N. Luxmore, in *Further Letters*, p. 395.   [6] "Escorial", st. 5.
[7] *E.g.*, Edmund Yates, *Recollections and Experiences*, 1884, I. 64;
Marcus Clarke, quoted by Brian Elliott, *Marcus Clarke*, 1958, pp.
15-24, 255, etc.
[8] *Poems*, pp. 14, 52, 66, 106; cp. *Correspondence*, p. 12.

A second poetic distinction came to Hopkins while he was still at school, when he had a poem printed in *Once a Week*. Its title, "Winter with the Gulf Stream",[9] points to an unusually mild season. When he left Highgate School two months later, it was as Governor's Gold Medallist and as the school's Exhibitioner to Balliol College, Oxford.

In his early undergraduate days Hopkins was planning a career in art or poetry, yet his first duty seemed to him to obtain the best possible degree.[10] He immersed himself in his classical studies with a devotion which left little time for verse, and if his flesh had not rebelled, leaving him feeling "idle" and unable to work, he would have pushed himself still harder. His private confession notes reveal the perfectionist standards in all things which he set himself, and his dissatisfaction over any "wasting" of time.

His earliest extant diary, a tiny book written in minute pencil, dates from September 1863. Its preoccupation with philology might puzzle those who did not realise that Moderations in those days concentrated upon verbal and formal matters.[11] Hopkins modulates from the classical shape of a word into English, citing Elizabethan and provincial usages which throw light upon the primary meanings. It is no accident that philological notes almost disappear from the diary after September 1864, the date of his Moderations—the important Part I examinations in which Hopkins achieved a First Class.

[9] Published 14 Feb. 1863; *Poems*, p. 12.

[10] *Further Letters*, pp. 214, 38, 230; *Letters*, p. 18.

[11] See Mark Pattison, *Suggestions on Academical Organisation*, Edinburgh 1868, pp. 271 ff. Among questions for Moderations were: "Mention and illustrate any technical meanings of the following words, connecting them with their original significance. . . ." (Easter 1864); and "Give instances of words to which a false derivation has been given by ancient writers: and show what advance has been made in the science of etymology through the comparison of several cognate languages. . . ." (Michaelmas 1864).

But though his conjectural etymologies had been worked out primarily for examination purposes, they undoubtedly influenced the poetry he was later to write. Thus we find him in his diary linking *shear, shred, potsherd, shard, ploughshare* ("that which divides the soil"), *share* ("probably = divide"), *shire* ("a division of land?"), *shower* ("a fall of water in little shreds or divisions?"). And in his poetry he coupled the last two "cognates" in "The Wreck of the Deutschland", st. 34:

> A released shower, let flash to the shire, ...[12]

The diaries are indeed rich in the raw material for verse. This was often specifically gathered for that purpose—for example:

Notes for poetry. Feathery rows of young corn. Ruddy, furred and branchy tops of the elms backed by rolling cloud. Frieze of sculpture, long-membered vines tugged at by reaching pursuant fauns.[13]

Immediately beneath this entry we have a first draft of his poem "Easter Communion":

> Ye whom the East
> With draught of thin and *pursuant* cold so nips,
> Breathe Easter now.[14]

When years later he came to write "Duns Scotus's Oxford", he incorporated another of these discovered words in the opening line:

> Towering city, and *branchy* between towers . . . .[15]

Besides containing the ingredients for poetry, the diaries include talented little sketches—many of them well reproduced in the modern edition of his *Journals*.[16]

[12] *J.P.*, p. 12; *Poems*, p. 62; cp. *J.P.*, p. 231.
[13] *J.P.*, p. 57.   [14] My italics; cp. *Poems*, p. 21.
[15] *Poems*, p. 79; my italics.
[16] *J.P.*, between pp. 456 and 457.

His aesthetic interests bring sparkle to the long Platonic Dialogue "On the Origin of Beauty"[17] which he produced after two years at Oxford. But one notices in his sketches a characteristic limitation in the subjects which occupied his pencil. Turning over the plates reproduced in the *Journals*, or examining the minor marginalia in the manuscript diaries, we see that he is absorbed in detail to the exclusion of the whole—in the pointed tracery of ecclesiastical windows, rather than the balanced church; in a mass of foliage or a tangle of weeds, every leaf individually acknowledged; in a fragment of cliff or a few limbs of tree, instead of a landscape composed and finished. His art is analytical. This painstaking technique was in keeping with the fashion; and, in a letter to Baillie,[18] Hopkins spoke of himself as sketching a good deal in a Ruskinesque manner. He went on:

> I have particular periods of admiration for particular things in Nature; for a certain time I am astonished at the beauty of a tree, shape, effect etc, then when the passion, so to speak, has subsided, it is consigned to my treasury of explored beauty, and acknowledged with admiration and interest ever after, while something new takes its place in my enthusiasm. The present fury is the ash, and perhaps barley and two shapes of growth in leaves and one in tree boughs and also a conformation of fine-weather cloud.

These were classes of objects to which Ruskin had devoted much close exposition in his *Modern Painters*. Ruskin set out to discover the subtle *laws* which produced particular shapes in a frond of leaves, that gave to the trunk or bough of a tree its special grace, or which characterised clouds into distinct and recognisable families. In selecting as an example of natural symmetry the fan of a chestnut, Hopkins echoed Ruskin in his

[17] *J.P.*, pp. 86-114, from a notebook dated 12 May 1865.
[18] 10 Jul. 1863; *Further Letters*, p. 202.

section "Of Leaf Beauty".[19] It is true that in February 1865 he entered *Modern Painters* in a list of "Books to be read". But it is plain that he means "read thoroughly". "Wordsworth" is on the same list, along with "Bacon's Essays", which Hopkins already knew well enough to parody with tolerable skill.[20] Hopkins in his early *Journals* even repeats the word which Ruskin most commonly used to explain the "ideal form" assumed by a species—namely the "law" of its shape.[21]

In his dialogue "On the Origin of Beauty", Hopkins makes his Professor of Aesthetics expound the theory which the poet later embodied in the word "inscape":

> although a leaf might have an outline on one side so irregular that no law could be traced in it, yet if the other side exactly agreed with it, you would say there was law or regularity about the leaf to make one side like the other.[22]

Here "law" means little more than the "generalised pattern characteristic of a particular thing", for which Hopkins looked wherever he went. These inscapes often lay purely on the surface, and were not outcrops from some deep under-lying philosophical reef of being. He found order even in "random clods and broken heaps of snow made by the cast of a broom".[23] Gazing down from a theatre box on the pit crowded with heads and shirt-fronts all facing one way, he found the "visible law" in the hundredfold repetition of white blobs upon black, the gashes of eyes and mouth, each seen to be individualised if looked at separately, but all conforming to a fundamental design:

[19] Ruskin, *Modern Painters*, Pt. VI, 4; cp. *J.P.*, p. 87.

[20] *J.P.*, pp. 56, 20, 13; *Further Letters*, pp. 208-9.

[21] See, *e.g.*, Ruskin's *Modern Painters*, Pt. II, 1. 2. 7., and Pt. VI, ch. iii; cp. *J.P.*, pp. 27, 90, 92, 139, 142, 146. See also my paper "Hopkins among the Victorians: Form in Art and Nature".

[22] *J.P.*, p. 90; cp. p. 199, where he speaks of the "inscape" of a chestnut tree. [23] *J.P.*, p. 230.

I could find a sort of beauty in this, certainly character
—but in fact that is almost synonymous with finding
order, anywhere.[24]

It is useful to compare Ruskin's chapters on cloud forms
with a remark such as the following from Hopkins's
Journals:

Those tretted mossy clouds have their law more in
helices, wave-tongues, than in anything else and it is
pretty perceptible.[25]

Ruskin tried to interpret shapes with the eye of a
scientist. He sought in geology the explanation of the
outlines which mountains of particular composition
assumed under the wear and stress of the elements; he
saw the action of heated air currents over hilly country
as the key to upsurging pillow clouds. Hopkins's initial
debt to Ruskin over law and inscape in nature calls for
open acknowledgment, explaining as it does the trend of
his observing, and even in his early choice of subjects to
sketch and describe.

But later Hopkins preferred his own invented term
"inscape" to "law", speaking, for example, of the beauty
of inscape shown in the rudely arched timberframes and
tiebeams of a barn.[26] As he deepened his study of philosophy and theology, and particularly as he probed into
the obscure treasures of Duns Scotus, he began to find a
more organic and spiritual inscape which was no mere
external generalisation of appearance, but which was in
truth the outward and visible landscape of an inward
state or instress. The "instress" within an object was its
"self" or nature, the "determining, selfmaking power"

[24] *J.P.*, p. 139.
[25] *J.P.*, p. 142.
[26] *J.P.*, p. 221 (19 Jul. 1872); cp. ref. to the "inscape of drapery"
in paintings seen in the National Gallery, *J.P.*, p. 241.

within it which left its mark on its external features; it was its spiritual energy or pitch of being.[27]

When Hopkins abandoned painting as a possible career, he did so partly because he foresaw moral dangers in its pursuit:

> The fact is that the higher and more attractive parts of the art put a strain upon the passions which I shd. think it unsafe to encounter.[28]

His private confession notes, kept before his conversion to the Roman Catholic Church, underline the temptations against which he waged a determined containing battle. "The Alchemist in the City" seems to be an allegory of an Oxford man's efforts to find spiritual wealth through his laborious classical study, and of the fated futility of his search. Looking back years later he echoed a friend's remark: "What philosophy good *or* bad —what *system*—did we ever learn at Oxford?"[29] The pressure of foredoomed failure—seriously misplaced, as we can now judge—was crushing the undergraduate at Oxford as it later did the professor at Dublin. Watching the crowds go about their labours, the young man cried:

> They do not waste their meted hours,
> But men and masters plan and build . . . .[30]

just as in middle age he was to lament:

> birds build—but not I build: no, but strain
> Time's eunuch, and not breed one work that wakes.[31]

"The Alchemist in the City" holds anticipations of other notes too. Mark especially the deep-set feeling of in-

[27] *S.D.W.*, p. 125; cp. *S.D.W.*, p. 168, where "commandments", "instress", and "laws" are again (1882) brought together. For a fine and detailed interpretation of "inscape" and "instress", supported by numerous examples from Hopkins's works, see Fr W. A. M. Peters, *Gerard Manley Hopkins* (1948), ch. 1.

[28] *Further Letters*, p. 231.   [29] *Further Letters*, p. 250.
[30] *Poems*, p. 24; *J.P.*, p. 62.   [31] *Poems*, p. 107.

H B

feriority which infuses this stanza of May 1865 even after we have made some allowance for the ostensible dramatic projection of character:

> Yet it is now too late to heal
> The incapable and cumbrous shame
> Which makes me when with men I deal
> More powerless than the blind or lame.[32]

The *Union Review* printed a highly metaphysical poem by Hopkins, "Barnfloor and Winepress", in 1865:

> Where the upper mill-stone roof'd His head,
> At morn we found the heavenly Bread.[33]

We might well have expected Hopkins to have attempted the Newdigate, emulating the success of Peter Worsley; but although he made a note in his diary of the closing date, 31 March 1864, and although we can recognise in subsequent notes some last-minute reading towards its unnamed subject ("The Relations of Civilised and Uncivilised Races"), he does not seem to have entered.[34] Indeed, his Oxford poetry is impressive neither in bulk nor (on the whole) quality. A curious paradox asserts itself: the only really telling pieces are religious, and yet his religious conscience was restraining him from composition. Not that he regarded his writing of poetry as sinful: but with Hopkins the good had always to give place to the better. The "habit of perfection" was growing on him; and where he heard duty's voice, its claims were paramount.

It is true that this imperative came partially from the obligation he felt upon him to obtain a good class. In the "preoccupied time of reading for the schools" he resolved "to have nothing to do with versemaking".[35] But a more

---

[32] *Poems*, p. 25; cp. "Trees by their Yield", p. 169.

[33] *Union Review*, III (1865), p. 579; *Poems*, p. 16. For draft (1864), see *Note-books*, p. 24.   [34] *J.P.*, pp. 20 ff.

[35] *Further Letters*, pp. 38, 230—cp. *Letters*, p. 18.

complicated mental state is shown by two private entries in the *Journal*:

> Nov. 6 [1865]. On this day by God's grace I resolved to give up all beauty until I had His leave for it.[36]

And then under January 1866:

> For Lent. No pudding on Sundays. No tea except if to keep me awake and then without sugar. Meat only once a day. No verses in Passion Week or on Fridays.[37]

So we find that poetry is becoming suspect: it is one of the luxuries of life which a good Christian should be prepared to sacrifice, along with sugar and pudding. The sources of this classification we will discuss later. He expresses his abnegation in the finest of his early poems, "The Habit of Perfection":

> Shape nothing, lips; be lovely-dumb:
> It is the shut, the curfew sent
> From there where all surrenders come
> Which only makes you eloquent.[38]

At Oxford his doubts concerning the validity of the Church of England, of which he was a most conscientious member, increased month by month. Many of his friends were torn by similar fears and questionings, as generations of Oxford men had been since the days of Newman's dramatic conversion to the Roman Catholic Church twenty years earlier. The spiritual gloom through which Hopkins was passing was reflected in his poems of 1865 and 1866. However we may attempt to explain it, we must admit a surprising degree of affinity in tone (though with significant differences) between the expression of his struggle of soul during his Oxford days and his last poems written in Ireland.

[36] *J.P.*, p. 71.
[37] *J.P.*, p. 72.
[38] *Poems*, p. 31.

> My prayers must meet a brazen heaven
> And fail or scatter all away . . .[39]

he wrote in 1865. Twenty years later he repeated his
plaint with greater urgency and in a style all his own:

> my lament
> Is cries countless, cries like dead letters sent
> To dearest him that lives alas! away.[40]

Newman's *Apologia pro vita sua*, setting out the agonising mental stages of his pilgrimage to Rome, had been
published in Hopkins's second year at Oxford, and had
created a new wave of self-examination among the inner
group of High-Church undergraduates of whom Hopkins was one. He began attending confession, a practice
reintroduced at Oxford by the Anglican leaders, Dr
Pusey and Dr Liddon.[41] A new seriousness, a desire for
total surrender to God, became evident in his poetry.[42]
His verse had shown a sudden intensification of spiritual
power as early as March 1865. The torments of inde-
cision lasted for about a year before he finally took the
step of entering the Church of Rome.[43] The resolution
affected the whole channelling of his energies. In successive steps separated by intervals of heart-searching, he
resolved to become a priest, then to enter one of the
closed religious orders, and finally to seek for admission
to the Society of Jesus,[44] one of the most exacting paths
he could have chosen. His new devotion to God brought
to a climax the old conflict between his desire for the
austere way of the saint, and his natural immersion in
beauty and poetry. Hopkins's asceticism went very deep:
it was not something imposed by his vows of obedience
as a Jesuit. Even at school and university, as is evident

---

[39] *Poems*, p. 27; cp. p. 32.   [40] *Poems*, p. 101.
[41] *J.P.*, pp. 54, 322, 71.   [42] See esp. *Poems*, pp. 26, 31.
[43] *Further Letters*, pp. 27, 397; *Letters*, pp. 6, 232; *J.P.*, p. 133, etc.
[44] *J.P.*, pp. 165-6.

from the comments of his fellow students, he had shown an exceptional power of physical austerity—witness his own "Easter Communion",[45] written in the Lent of 1865. Long before he had become a priest, he had begun worrying about the part which poetry could play in his new existence.

> I want to write still [he remarked in February 1868], and as a priest I very likely can do that too, not so freely as I shd. have liked, e.g. nothing or little in the verse way, but no doubt what wd. best serve the cause of my religion.[46]

But the pull towards poetry was so strong that it threatened, as he told Bridges, to "interfere with my state and vocation"[47]; therefore, after pondering the matter for some nine months, he resolved to burn his poems as a symbolic act, very much as St Francis of Assisi stripped himself of his worldly clothes at the start of his new life.

This seems to be the meaning of Hopkins's enigmatic reference to his "slaughter of the Innocents".[48] Up to this point his writing of verse had belonged to the category of neutral acts, neither good nor bad, winning him no merit and not advancing the cause of the Catholic Church. His poems were "innocent" indeed, but their slaughter marked in decisive ceremony the surrender to God of his long-cherished desire to become known as a poet. He told Bridges that he had saved corrected copies of a few things, and (no doubt realising that these might some day be wanted) he promised to send them to him for safe keeping.[49] Their fate was no longer to be his own care. As for the future, he resolved "to write no more, as not belonging to my profession, unless it were by the wish of my superiors".[50] The fact that so much of his earlier

---

[45] *Poems*, p. 20; cp. *Further Letters*, pp. 23, 434.
[46] To Baillie, *Further Letters*, p. 231.   [47] *Letters*, p. 24.
[48] *J.P.*, p. 165; cp. pp. 152, 164, and House's Appendix, p. 537.
[49] *Letters*, p. 24.   [50] *Correspondence*, p. 14.

poetry survived has aroused suspicion as to the sincerity
of this "deliberate holocaust".[51] But it would have been
ostentatious to have written to all who had copies of his
verse asking that every trace of them should be destroyed.
The threat to his religious vocation lay, not in the poems
themselves, but in the risk of his attachment to them:
hence their sacramental burning, an action which
appears to have been frequently misinterpreted.

From that point until over seven years later Hopkins
seems to have virtually limited his composition to works
which his Rectors asked for—a congratulatory address
to a new bishop, May verses such as were placed on the
statue of the Virgin at Stonyhurst for her festival, and a
litany.[52] But this fallow interval was of immense benefit
to his poetry. For one thing, it allowed time for the old
conventional crop to be rooted out, leaving the soil fertile
for an entirely new strain. For another, these were years
during which he matured and intensified in thought.
Most important of all, in the course of his duties as a
teacher, he was led to think out the basis of classical and
English prosody, and to develop a new rhythm, the hints
of which he had given Bridges in his "Lines for a Picture
of St. Dorothea".[53]

Hopkins left Oxford in the middle of 1867 with a first-
class honours degree. Having decided in the spring of
1868 to join the Society of Jesus in autumn, he gave July
to an exhilarating walking tour in Switzerland with a
friend, an experience which produced some of the most
animated pages of his *Journal*.[54]

Hopkins's life in the Society of Jesus may be split
into three divisions: his lengthy period of study; a brief
spell of three years as a parish priest (though to him they
seemed interminably long); and his various teaching

---

[51] House, quoted in *Poems*, 3rd. edn., ed. W. H. Gardner, p. 278.
[52] *Further Letters*, pp. 238, 122, 134. See *Poems*, pp. 37, 38, and
perhaps Nos. 167-70, all undated.
[53] *Letters*, p. 24.   [54] *J.P.*, pp. 168-84.

posts, nearly always in senior positions, culminating in his appointment as Professor of Classics in the Royal University in Dublin. First came two years of spiritual training as a novice, designed to mould him in the ways of the Society of Jesus and of absolute obedience to the will of God as this was made known to him. His novitiate was spent (7 Sep. 1868 to 9 Sep. 1870) at Manresa House, Roehampton, which, like the two other Jesuit houses in which Hopkins was privileged to receive his training, was situated amongst scenery which nourished the poet within him. Manresa House stood in its own extensive grounds, laid out with trees which Hopkins came to love—Turkey-oaks, limes, a Spanish chestnut, elms and wych-elms, and a huge mulberry in which Hopkins was sent climbing to pick the fruit.[55] He grieved when storms or felling thinned their ranks. The house looked out on to the gleaming green or dusty velvet of the Great Park at Richmond, not a building in view for miles except for the White Lodge half buried in a wood.[56]

In September 1870, his novitiate over, he took his first vows and was transferred direct to the three-year course of philosophy which formed the normal third stage of a Jesuit's training. The scene of this was much wilder, at St Mary's Hall, Stonyhurst, among the Lancashire fells and cloughs—a "beautiful range of moors dappled with light and shade" (though beneath soot-laden clouds), and wonderful rivers rippling golden-brown, deep among wooded banks. Just as his philosophy was completed, there arose a need for someone to conduct the advanced rhetoric courses at Manresa House for the "junior scholastics", among whom were some preparing for University of London degrees. Hopkins was given this senior teaching post for a year (28 Aug. 1873 to 28 Aug. 1874)—

[55] *J.P.*, pp. 189, 192, 196, etc.
[56] A plan of the grounds and full description of the buildings as they were when the Novitiate first moved there is given in *Letters and Notices* (1861).

a responsibility he accepted with much misgiving, but to the great benefit of his knowledge of English poetic rhythm.[57] Thereafter his studies were resumed—three years of theology in Wales leading to his ordination in the autumn of 1877. It was during this period that he began writing poetry again after the years of self-restraint —a spell of renewed creative activity for which the charm of his new surroundings must take due credit. Foremost was the valley of the Elwy, upon which St Beuno's College looks down, with the Great Orms Head and Snowdon featuring the distance. "The instress and charm of Wales" gripped him from his very first week in the College.

It is unfortunate that his last known *Journal* breaks off in mid-sentence in February 1875, the year in which "The Wreck of the *Deutschland*" was to force itself into his poetic consciousness. The journals which have come to light are invaluable to the critic of his poetry: they show him treasuring up the discoveries he made during manual work in the fields, during summer holidays—in Devon or the Isle of Man—during the walks taken for recreation, though often damped by much less observant or receptive companions. His constant wish was to see things "freshly, as if my eye were still growing".[58] Every landscape held objects for visual exploration: he seldom had to record in his diary that although he had looked he "did not find out much".[59] We learn the inscapes of wild flowers, of big pack-clouds overhead, the radiating patterns of diminishing bubbles trapped in slabs of ice, the exact formation of knops and buds on an ash, set down in sentences in which the analysis of a scientist meets the verbal inventiveness of an artist. And once recorded, they were there to be called on in later years as he composed verse, sometimes with striking reliance upon the very phrases of his prose, at others adapting the

[57] See *J.P.*, pp. 267-90.
[58] *J.P.*, pp. 228, 231.   [59] *J.P.*, p. 234.

insight or image to the needs of the poem in an inspired way.

A few entries from the summer of 1873 alone will provide various examples of the relationship between journals and poems. First some direct verbal connexions:

Painted white *cobbled foam* tumbling over the rocks and combed away off their sides again . . . . I saw big smooth *flinty waves* . . . . In an enclosure of rocks the peaks of the water *romped* and wandered.[60]

Turning to "The Wreck of the *Deutschland*" we read (the italics are again mine):

the sea *flint-flake*, black-backed in the regular blow. . . .

dandled the to and the fro
Through the *cobbled foam*-fleece. . . .

They fought with God's cold—
And they could not and fell to the deck
(Crushed them) or water (and drowned them) or rolled
With the *sea-romp* over the wreck.[61]

A neighbouring paragraph catches the thunderstorm which broke out one evening:

Flashes lacing two clouds above or the cloud and the earth started upon the eyes in live veins of rincing or riddling liquid white, inched and jagged as if it were the shivering of a bright riband string which had once been kept bound round a blade and danced back into its pleatings.[62]

This tallies closely with the explanation, sent to Bridges, of his poem "The Sea and the Skylark":

[60] *J.P.*, 235-6.
[61] "The Wreck of the *Deutschland*", sts. 13, 16 (Ms. A), 17.
[62] *J.P.*, p. 233.

The skein and coil are the lark's song, which from his height gives the impression (not to me only) of something falling to the earth and not vertically quite but tricklingly or wavingly, something as a skein of silk ribbed by having been tightly wound on a narrow card or a notched holder . . . : the laps or folds are the notes or short measures and bars of them.[63]

We might further note that this connexion between lightning rinsing the air and the song of a bird is explicitly made in "Spring":

thrush

Through the echoing timber does so rinse and wring
The ear, it strikes like lightnings to hear him sing.[64]

As a novice during his first two years in the Society, his attention was almost completely absorbed in meditations around the *Spiritual Exercises of St Ignatius* and kindred books. Contact with the outside world—indeed even with other novices and juniors—was both officially and voluntarily reduced to a minimum. He could not see the daily newspapers, or follow the literary journals, or read new volumes of poetry as they appeared, or correspond freely on such topics with his friends.[65] Always wrestling with his nature and seeking for greater sanctity, Hopkins seems to have imposed on himself (though probably with the permission of his spiritual directors) a six months' penance which prevented him from studying the cycles of leaf and flower, or mapping in words the configuration of the clouds, from 25 January to 25 July 1869.[66] It may be taken as most unlikely that this was an external edict from the Master of Novices. Sacrificing

---

[63] *Letters*, p. 164.   [64] *Poems*, p. 67.
[65] I draw here on ms. journals and weekly notice-books kept at Manresa during the 1870s and 80s; cp. *Letters*, pp. 30-1, when he was a theology student.   [66] *J.P.*, p. 190.

what gave him most spontaneous pleasure, Hopkins de-
liberately carried out the aspirations which he had
framed even before he had formally joined the Catholic
Church:

> Be shelled, eyes, with blinding dark
> To look on the uncreated Light;
> The coloured shows which else you mark
> Tangle and break the field of sight.[67]

That the penance was self-imposed appears the more
probable when we examine a parallel instance which
occurred when he was Professor of Rhetoric at Manresa.
On the way to Windsor one lovely harvest holiday, he
rejoiced in the "beautiful blushing yellow in the straw of
the uncut ryefields", and the delicate ears of wheat gently
stirred by the breeze: "All this I would have looked at
again in returning but during dinner I talked too freely
and unkindly and had to do penance going home."[68]

A close study of all that Hopkins has left us indicates
time and again that in his scruples he went beyond anything which was laid down for him, and even tended to
reject concessions which his Rectors designed to protect
his health and serenity.[69] This attitude was hard for his
non-Catholic friends to appreciate. Bridges remained
convinced that Hopkins, mistaking his true tempera-
ment, had signed away his liberty and been caught in
the grasp of a relentless system. It is true that the English
Province of the Society of Jesus in Hopkins's day was
somewhat under-developed on the aesthetic side: they
were so preoccupied with their main purpose of winning
England back to the Faith that they neglected to encourage the artistic gifts of one of their most original
members. But scrutiny of Hopkins's manuscripts and
printed works has completely convinced me that his

---

[67] Early version of "The Habit of Perfection", written 18-19
Jan. 1866, Ms. A. Cp. *Poems*, p. 31.
[68] *J.P.*, p. 249. [69] See, *e.g.*, *Letters*, p. 201 (1885).

comparative lack of productiveness stemmed from other causes—from his own long-standing "war within" (which contributed to his "melancholia"), from his natural diffidence and misgivings, above all from his high desire to achieve supererogatory merit through going the second mile when his poetic journey lay in the contrary direction.

The unostentatious good-humour with which Hopkins politely declined invitations to follow an easier path is well illustrated by an anecdote dating from the time when he was a full Professor of Classics in Dublin. Calling on a parish priest, the Rev. Father Wade, he was urged to stay for dinner. Father Hopkins replied that he had not obtained leave to dine out. "Oh! as to that," said Father Wade, "I will take the whole responsibility upon my-self." "That's all very well," came Hopkins's reply, "you may be Wade, but I should be found wanting!"[70]

The stairs up the pyramid of grace seem, from a secular point of view, to narrow exceedingly as they ascend. When Hopkins, a newly-converted Catholic, took up his first teaching post after graduating, he expressed an ardour to "read almost everything that has ever been written".[71] Alas, he soon allowed the demands of his fifth and sixth forms to impose a diet upon this in-tellectual zest, so that within six months he was lament-ing that an interest in philosophy (especially Aristotle) was almost the only one in which he felt himself still at liberty to indulge.[72] The note of conscience forms a recognisable undertone, though he had not yet decided to join a religious order. The official study of philosophy, when it came, however, proved laborious in itself: he wrote to an old Balliol friend:

[70] Obituary in *Letters and Notices*, xx (1890), p. 173, quoted from the account of a close friend; reprinted in *The Month* cxxxiv (1919), p. 158, and Fr Lahey, *Life*, pp. 145-6.

[71] *Further Letters*, p. 228 (15 Sep. 1867).

[72] *Further Letters*, p. 231 (12 Feb. 1868).

I am going through a hard course of scholastic logic
... which takes all the fair part of the day and leaves
one fagged at the end for what remains.[73]

He regretted that he had energy for very few general
books, and could read only in snatches. A few years later,
at St Beuno's for the next stage of his training, theology,
his prescribed tasks once more monopolised most of his
energy, and he reluctantly put back into the library
Aristotle's *Metaphysics*, feeling that he would now never
be able to read it. He consoled himself that he could still,
"at all events a little, read Duns Scotus".[74]

In Wales his proposal to study the Welsh language and
its literature was at first rebuffed because it was not
"purely for the sake of labouring among the Welsh".[75]
Fortunately the discouragement was later withdrawn,
and he was permitted to take Welsh lessons—the only
one in the Welsh College of St Beuno's doing so—to the
immense enrichment of his subsequent poetry. At Manresa House the books in English literature and criticism
had been inadequate, so that a successor to Hopkins's
post as lecturer in rhetoric had to make regular visits to
the British Museum Library in order to prepare his
course.[76] No wonder Hopkins lamented that he had
taught rhetoric "so badly and so painfully".[77] Later, as
a parish priest, Hopkins confessed from time to time that
he had been unable, either through dearth of leisure or
library facilities, to look up even well-known works such
as Coleridge's Preface to *Christabel*.[78]

Yet this degree of insulation from the poetry of his own
day protected the surge of his own originality. Even as
an undergraduate his reading had been limited, not by

---

[73] *Further Letters*, p. 234 (10 Apr. 1871).
[74] *Letters*, p. 31 (20 Feb. 1875); cp. *Further Letters*, pp. 131, 143.
[75] *J.P.*, p. 258.
[76] Ms. *Rhetoricians' Journal* (1878-80), Manresa House.
[77] *Letters*, p. 30.
[78] *Correspondence*, pp 21, 30; cp. *Further Letters*, pp. 148-9, 243.

the absence of many-sided curiosity, but by the minute attention which he had focussed upon the classical texts prescribed for Greats: he had not kept up with the works which most influenced his contemporaries.[79] Although his poetry is Victorian rather than modern in numerous ways, the few friends who read it found it shockingly new and untutored, as though it had come from some isolated literary Mount Athos. Yet his instincts seem to us, looking back from the twentieth century, so unerring as to direct his judgments and practice always in the right direction. Hopkins's letters of literary criticism come from his later days, not the formative years before "The Wreck of the *Deutschland*". Even so, a surprising proportion of his comments bypass the novels and poems of the greater world to dwell on the lesser poetry of his three friends, Robert Bridges, R. W. Dixon, and Coventry Patmore.

The outburst of Hopkins's revolutionary poetry which came at St Beuno's after 1875 was the product of various forces—of a sense of spiritual elation which he lacked both earlier and later, a concentration of interest which his hard professional studies had induced in him, and the year of authorised attention to English and classical literature which he had recently spent at Manresa House, preparing students for such examinations as the University of London pass and honours degrees in English and classics. His surviving notes which seem to have been made for this purpose, on "Rhythm and Other Structural Parts of Rhetoric",[80] show him establishing or reinforcing the bases on which his theory of sprung rhythm was presently to be built. But no theory can account for genius: "The Wreck of the *Deutschland*" breaks upon most students even today as a poem for which their previous reading has left them totally unprepared.

The story of how the "Wreck" came to be written is

[79] *Further Letters*, p. 230.
[80] *J.P.*, pp. 267-90, including two pages on "Poetry and Verse".

well known. A general persecution of the closed religious orders on the Continent had been proceeding for some time: one by one, priests and nuns had been harried out of Germany for refusal to accept the authority of the Government in religious matters, and although some of them had braved imprisonment in order to return secretly to minister to their abandoned flocks, most had been compelled into exile. Hopkins was much moved by the harsh treatment to which Catholic peasants in Poland and elsewhere were being subjected.[81] The Jesuit journal *The Month* had featured the persecution in Europe in successive numbers, relating stories of suffering or courage. It did not, however, record the fate of the five Franciscan nuns, sailing into exile in the *Deutschland*, who were drowned when their vessel was wrecked in a terrible storm in December 1875. On Hopkins this event made a deep impression, more acute than any other wreck or the still more serious loss of life in three colliery explosions in that "week of disasters".[82] He spoke to his Rector, who expressed the wish that

someone would write a poem on the subject. On this hint I set to work and, though my hand was out at first, produced one. I had long had haunting my ear the echo of a new rhythm which now I realised on paper.[83]

Here was not merely permission to write—rather a virtual request from his superior. And the resulting poem was no mere narrative, but an act of devotion, a sermon in verse to "startle the poor sheep back".[84] It was the work of a man whose profession was not poetry but the

---

[81] *Further Letters*, pp. 132-3 (24 Apr. 1875).

[82] *Further Letters*, p. 135; leading article, *Illustrated London News*, 11 Dec. 1875, p. 570.

[83] To Dixon, 5 Oct. 1878, *Correspondence*, p. 14; see Ritz, *Le Poète Gérard Manley Hopkins*, p. 180, n. 25.

[84] "The Wreck of the *Deutschland*", st. 31.

priesthood. Nevertheless, the story of the wreck is told with an artistic power gathered through years of watching and feeling.

Even today readers find the "Wreck" so unlike any other poetry to which they have become familiarised as to require special application for its perusal. But to his fellow Jesuits the rhythm and expression seemed not experimental but incompetent. Hopkins tried reading parts of it aloud to his fellow "theologian", C. W. Barraud (a priest who was himself later to be known as a poet and dramatist), with whom he had joyfully bathed in St Winefred's Well.[85] Forty-three years later Fr Barraud could still remember how he abandoned hope of following the "Wreck". When Hopkins's *Poems* appeared in its first edition in 1918, Fr Barraud in an article in *The Month* castigated the wilfulness with which his friend had "set all tradition at defiance", so that

the more he laboured at his subject the more obscure it became. Yet he did not repent. . . . It has been said —he used to say it himself—that his verses need for proper appreciation to be read aloud by one who has mastered their eccentricities. Well, I heard the bard himself read parts of *The Wreck of the Deutschland*, which he was writing at the time, and could understand hardly one line of it.[86]

Hopkins might have been warned by this lack of comprehension among his cultured friends, but when his mother suggested that she might help to have the poem published, Hopkins wrote back with an innocent professional complacency:

[85] *J.P.*, p. 261.

[86] *The Month*, 134 (Aug. 1919), pp. 158-9. The article is signed only "C.B.", and not identified in the publisher's key index, or by E. J. Mellown (1965). But the writer reveals that he had studied philosophy and theology with Hopkins, and that he later went to Demerara (in British Guiana). These facts, together with the ref. in *J.P.*, p. 261, seem to me to point to Fr Clement Barraud.

You forget that we have a magazine of our own, the *Month*. I have asked Fr. Coleridge the editor, who is besides my oldest friend in the Society, to take it.[87]

The Month was at that time venturing only the simplest religious verse on its readers, such as this (from June 1876):

> Oh, that our souls were gardens
> Of flowers most sweet and rare,
> All watered with tears of penance,
> And nourished with faithful prayer!

Fr Coleridge was therefore taking a bold step when, after some delay, he promised to print the "Wreck" in the number for August 1876, provided that the metrical accents with which the poet had marked the manuscript in blue chalk were dispensed with.[88] This condition may have proved fatal: Hopkins felt that readers would never follow the unusual rhythms without aid, and unless they did, he considered that the poem would fail. Whether they would follow them even with such help seemed to the editor dubious, and this opinion has been confirmed by Sydney Smith (another of Hopkins's fellow theologians), to whom he handed the manuscript with its diacritical signs, he delayed printing it from number to number and finally returned it unused.[89]

How serious the rejection was to be for the poet's newly-released gift Hopkins did not at first realise. For expenditure of time on poetry to be fully justified—the "Wreck" seems to have taken him about six months to compose[90]—the poems would have to exert an influence for his Church which only publication could give them. The disappointment was softened for him by the printing of another poem that same year, "The Silver Jubilee", which appeared above his initials at the end of Fr Morris's panegyric on the twenty-fifth year of the episco-

[87] *Further Letters*, p. 138. [88] *Further Letters*, pp. 138-9.
[89] *J.P.*, p. 382. [90] *Further Letters*, pp. 138-9.

H C

pate of the Roman Catholic Bishop of Shrewsbury, Dr
James Brown.[91] Fortunately Hopkins could not realise
at the time that such comparatively uncomplicated
verses were the only ones likely to receive official accept-
ance, and he began to produce sonnets and poems as
inspiration took him. When disillusionment at length fell,
he did not blame the Society for its lack of appreciation
and encouragement. Like a true son of the Church, he
questioned within himself whether he had been right to
go on with works which failed (through lack of currency)
to achieve their original purpose of striking a blow for
his cause—while creating in himself, a priest, a "preoccupation of the mind which belonged to more sacred
or more binding duties".[92]

Although "The Wreck of the *Deutschland*" remained
unpublished, not only during Hopkins's lifetime, but until nearly thirty years after his death, the fact that it had
been asked for by this Rector liberated Hopkins from his
self-imposed ban upon poetry. "After writing this I held
myself free to compose," he told Dixon two years later,
"but cannot find it in my conscience to spend time upon
it."[93] It is curious that the three other poems which
greeted the summer of 1876 are among the few which
Hopkins wrote as a priest without a religious drive behind them: "Penmaen Pool", composed for the visitors'
book at the George Inn, near the Society's holiday villa
at Barmouth[94]; the unfinished "Moonrise"; and "The
Woodlark", skilfully put together from the manuscript
draft by Fr Bliss, s.j. He may, in fact, have abandoned
the last two, as well as other nature poems, when he
found them not susceptible of spiritual application.

[91] *Further Letters*, p. 140; *Poems*, p. 63. See A. Thomas, s.j., "G. M.
Hopkins and the Silver Jubilee Album".

[92] *Correspondence*, p. 88.

[93] To Dixon, 5 Oct. 1878, *Correspondence*, p. 15.

[94] A visit to the George Inn up the Barmouth Estuary was then,
as since, one of the regular highlights of the fortnight's holiday
enjoyed by theologians and other students.

To his third year at St Beuno's, however, belong poems in which the themes of the Creator and His creation are most satisfactorily blended, such as "God's Grandeur", "The Starlight Night", and "The Wind-hover". If he had been allowed to stay in Wales at St Beuno's after his ordination for a fourth year of theology, we may suppose that these happy poems would have continued. Even though he had found no kindred spirits there to share his tastes in poetry or his feeling for Welsh,[95] the country itself was congenial: valleys, mountains, and meadows of Wales stirred him as no other setting except Oxford was to do. It was a great disappointment to him to find his confident expectation of a fourth year at St Beuno's denied in favour of a spell of "nondescript" work at Mount Saint Mary, a boys' school near Chesterfield.[96] The Provincial's decision not to promote Hopkins to a year of advanced study may have been due to the strain this could have imposed on his health, as well as his supposed lack of aptitude for theology.[97] As a preacher, moreover, he tended to irradi-ate some picturesque angle of his text in imaginative style, instead of throwing the main structure into bold relief. Thus the poetic passages of a trial sermon preached be-fore his fellow theologians amid the distractions of the refectory six months before his ordination were lost upon them. With quaint vividness of detail he portrayed the crowd at the Feeding of the Five Thousand, divided into strict groups of fifty, the "joyous green grass of that spring plotted with flowerbeds of human limbs and faces".[98]

[95] *Further Letters*, pp. 140, 147.

[96] *Further Letters*, p. 148. On the expected fourth year of theology, see *Letters*, pp. 30, 43; *Further Letters*, pp. 122, 242; and Fr Devlin's wise comments, *S.D.W.*, p. xiii.

[97] See Downes, *Gerard Manley Hopkins*, pp. 22, 13; cp. *Letters*, p. 31, and *Further Letters*, p. 143.

[98] *S.D.W.*, pp. 225-33. The Greek original in Mk VI.40 must have stimulated him: *prasia* means lit. "garden bed".

To the disappointment over the rejection of his poetry were thus added growing fears lest he might fail to justify his place in the Society of Jesus, in which he had now taken his final vows as a priest. Nothing could have grieved him more deeply: in comparison with this profession his place as a poet weighed little in his esteem.[99] But these two regions of failure inevitably lay in the same belt of depression. Thus the year 1878 brought with it two blights. In the literary field, another major religious poem, "The Loss of the *Eurydice*", was also rejected by *The Month*, although Hopkins had made it "simpler, shorter, and without marks".[100] In the religious sphere he had been modestly gratified when Fr Gallwey had particularly asked that Hopkins might become one of his special preachers at the fashionable London Farm Street Church, and the poet had assumed that he would be there permanently or at least for a substantial time.[101] But forgetting and flurry marred the delivery of a sermon in August; and, when he was moved after only five months, he must have suspected that he had not fulfilled the confidence of the Rector, whom he had long known and admired.

Hopkins's next post might seem to an outsider to have been attractive indeed: he was sent to the Jesuit parish of St Aloysius in Oxford. But this newly-opened church had aroused great anti-Catholic feeling, as is evinced by a revealing and hitherto overlooked letter in the *Oxford and Cambridge Undergraduate Journal*.[102] Shortly before Hopkins arrived, a correspondent lamented that nearly two thousand immature young students were being exposed to a "staff of clever controversialists . . . whose only reason for being in Oxford is their singular skill in argument, persuasion and propagandism". Pointing to the

---

[99] *Correspondence*, p. 28.
[100] *Correspondence*, p. 15; cp. *Letters*, p. 66.
[101] *Further Letters*, p. 150; *Letters*, p. 55.
[102] 13 Jun. 1878.

new presbytery being built, the writer continued: "In a few weeks it will be inhabited by a band of brethren, whose sole object is to guide men of money, or weak brains, or both, into the Romish haven of rest and peace." The "band" of Jesuits consisted of Fr Hopkins alone, sent to work under Fr Parkinson!

The diffident new priest kept himself aloof from the undergraduates: indeed his time was more than fully occupied with the Cowley Barracks (to which his Rector had been appointed Chaplain), and with the Catholic tradesmen and artisans.[103]

Hopkins's personality did not blend well with that of the priest-in-charge at Oxford, nor would his avoidance of all unnecessary contact with the University itself have recommended him as the ideal man for the post. So once again he was moved on, after a spell of duty which, being less than a year, was much below what he could have expected. In his next parish, Bedford Leigh, he was more at home, the comforting warmth of the people compensating for the smoke-ridden atmosphere:

it is sweet to be a little flattered. . . . Now these Lanca-shire people of low degree or not of high degree are those who most have seemed to me to welcome me and make much of me.[104]

He felt he was needed. *"Felix Randal"*,[105] a portrait of the relationship between priest and parishioner, rather than of the blacksmith himself, is perhaps the most successful of a number of poems written about this time in which Hopkins was drawing upon professional experience—"The Bugler's First Communion", "The Handsome Heart", "At the Wedding March", and "Brothers".[106]

---

[103] See Fr. C. C. Martindale, S.J., *Catholics in Oxford*, Oxford (Blackwells 1925), and Fr. A. Bischoff, S.J., *St Aloysius 1875-1955*, London (O.U.P.) 1955. [104] *Letters*, p. 97; *Further Letters*, pp. 243, 245. [105] *Poems*, p. 86. [106] *Poems*, pp. 81, 82, 86, 87.

From Bedford Leigh, where he had been merely re-
lieving for three months, Hopkins was moved to Liverpool, where he was allowed to preach in the crowded and
fashionable Church of St Francis Xavier on four successive Sunday evenings immediately after he arrived.[107]
But the boldness of his thought and phraseology gradu-
ally brought him a mild though hampering censorship.[108]

Let us quote from one of his early sermons, which he
entitled "The Fall of God's First Kingdom" until the
theological exactitude of the phrase was questioned, and
the printed titles were blanked out. The passage is not
only a display of the poet in the pulpit, but it reveals the
sources of his own hesitation about writing poetry. He is
picturing Eve wandering alone in the Garden of Eden,
with the tempter preparing the undoing of mankind:

Eve was alone. It was no sin to be alone, she was in
her duty, God had given her freedom and she was
wandering free, God had made her independent of her
husband and she need not be at his side. Only God
had made her for Adam's companion; it was her
office, her work, the reason of her being to companion
him and she was not doing it. There is no sin, but there
is no delicacy of duty, no zeal for the sovereign's honour, no generosity, no supererogation. And Adam, he
too was alone. He had been commanded to dress and
to keep Paradise. What flower, what fruitful tree, what
living thing was there in Paradise so lovely as Eve, so
fruitful as the mother of all flesh, that needed or could
repay his tendance and his keeping as she? There was
no sin; yet at the one fatal moment when of all the
world care was wanted care was not forthcoming, the
thing best worth keeping was unkept. And Eve stood
by the forbidden tree, which God had bidden them not
to eat of, which *she* said God had bidden them not even
touch; she neither sinned nor was tempted to sin by

[107] *S.D.W.*, pp. 50-68.   [108] *S.D.W.*, pp. 62, 68, 81, 83, 89.

standing near it, yet she would go to the very bounds
and utmost border of her duty. To do so was not
dangerous of itself, as it would be to us. When some
child, one of Eve's poor daughters, stands by a peach-
tree, eyeing the blush of colour on the fruit, fingering
the velvet bloom upon it, breathing the rich smell, and
in imagination tasting the sweet juice, the nearness, the
mere neighbourhood is enough to undo her, she looks
and is tempted, she touches and is tempted more, she
takes and tastes. But in Eve there was nothing of this;
she was not mastered by concupiscence, *she* mastered
it. There she stood, beautiful, innocent, with her
original justice *and with nothing else*, nothing to stain it,
but nothing to heighten and brighten it: she felt no
cravings, for she was mistress of herself and would not
let them rise; she felt no generous promptings, no lift-
ings of the heart to give God glory, for she was mistress
of herself and gave them no encouragement. Such was
Eve before her fall.[109]

Here we see Hopkins interpreting the Fall of Man as
springing from too confident a resting upon permitted
pleasures, instead of positive activity leading to God's
glory. Amusing ourselves, using our leisure in blameless
ways, admiring the stars, composing music—all these
were morally neutral or indifferent acts which laid up
no treasure in Heaven.[110] In his own evaluation of his
poetic gifts he seems to have misclassified his poetry as
something without positive merit—a calculation, alas,
influenced by the light esteem in which he felt the Society
itself held it.

When Hopkins told Bridges, "I cannot in conscience
spend time on poetry", he explained that he did not
mean to publish his verse unless the suggestion came

---

[109] *S.D.W.*, pp. 64-5.
[110] See *S.D.W.*, pp. 166-8, and Fr Devlin's note on the influence
of Duns Scotus here; cp. *Poems*, p. 185.

from his spiritual directors. But Hopkins diffidently
buried his talents and did not test the reaction of his
superiors: they were for the most part unaware that he
was a poet.

I have taken and mean to take no step [to publish]
beyond the attempt I made to print my two wrecks in
the *Month*. If some one in authority knew of my having
some poems printable and suggested my doing it I shd.
not refuse, I should be partly, though not altogether,
glad. But that is very unlikely. All therefore that I
think of doing is to keep my verses together in one
place—at present I have not even correct copies—,
that, if anyone shd. like, they might be published after
my death. And that again is unlikely, as well as
remote.[111]

Under such circumstances he thwarted the impulse to
write as being an inferior good. He confessed that he
lacked the "inducements and inspirations that make
others compose".[112]

An attitude which began in a desire to "seek first the
Kingdom of God", however, became entangled in his
human frailty, his lack of self-confidence. He found the
life he led in the Society "liable to many mortifications",
and he was in fear of any action which might appear a
"sort of insubordination".[113] When Canon Dixon, having
admired his poems in manuscript, sent "The Loss of the
Eurydice" to a newspaper, Hopkins withdrew it in agita-
tion lest some fellow Jesuits might see it and put a
wrong construction upon his having work published in
this fashion.[114] The sharp reaction of Hall Caine and
Dante Gabriel Rossetti to his least experimental sonnets,
as an unwarrantable distortion of the traditional verse
form, was a further setback: his "Starlight Night",
"Skylark", and "Andromeda" were returned unpub-

[111] *Letters*, p. 66.   [112] *Ibid.*
[113] *Correspondence*, p. 28.   [114] *Correspondence*, pp. 29-31.

lished.[115] He was further hurt by the use of the name "Gifted Hopkins" by Andrew Lang in widely-read articles in *The Saturday Review*, for the imaginary author of a book of unwanted poems, published at five shillings, only to be remaindered at fourpence. He could not believe that no oblique reference was intended to himself, in spite of Lang's reassurances.[116]

But his interest in poetry was kept alive through correspondence with four friends, Bridges, Dixon, Patmore, and Baillie, of whom the first three were themselves poets. With Bridges (who had known him since Oxford) he exchanged a long series of letters, in which each subjected the other's verse to magisterial criticism, accompanied (especially from Hopkins's side), with warm encouragement.[117] Bridges subsequently destroyed the letters he wrote to Hopkins: from Hopkins's rejoinders and Bridges's subsequent editorial notes in the First Edition of 1918, one gathers that they frequently showed impatience over his "oddness", "affectation", and "singularity", in poems where Hopkins was conscious only of "novelty and boldness".[118] This interest in his poetry was of the utmost value to Hopkins, but at times Bridges seems to have been unaware that his friend was in a state of mental prostration in which he could not benefit from well-intentioned advice. The sensitive Hopkins even reached the strange conviction that Bridges admired only his touches and found the general effect of his verse "repulsive".[119] The falsity of this impression is plainly evidenced by the intelligent care with which Bridges gathered his verse into one book, preserved all the manuscripts he could find after his death, and

---

[115] *Letters*, pp. 127-8; *Correspondence*, pp. 46-7. See E. W. Mellown, in *Notes and Queries*, n.s., VI (1959), pp. 109-110.

[116] *Letters*, pp. 153, 158-9, 161, 223-4, 294-5. The origin of "Gifted Hopkins" is explained by W. H. Pearson, *Notes and Queries*, n.s., VI (1959), pp. 452-3. [117] See *e.g.*, *Letters*, pp. 93-6, 121.

[118] *Letters*, pp. 38, 44-5, 54, 66, etc. [119] *Letters*, p. 137.

arranged for their eventual publication when the time seemed riper.[120] No one can read the volume of letters which Hopkins sent to Bridges without perceiving how much he needed his support, and how stimulating their mutual contact was to both of them.

A. W. Baillie had been a brilliant fellow-student at Balliol; his correspondence with Hopkins extends from 1863 till 1888. The other two friendships arose out of Hopkins's unselfish wish to save "neglected" poets whom he admired from sharing the heartache of feeling themselves forgotten. R. W. Dixon had taught him for one term when he had been a schoolboy at Highgate. Hopkins began the correspondence, at a time when he had himself abandoned hope of publication, with a generous tribute to Dixon's scarcely-known volumes of poetry. Their letters contain many fascinating literary judgments, and Dixon became one of his most encouraging allies. With Coventry Patmore, on the other hand, the virtue seems to have flowed almost exclusively one way: Patmore was too old and rigid in taste to accept Hopkins's innovations in metre, form, and thought. After battling with their sprung rhythm and complexity for some months, Patmore added his quota of disapprobation:

It seems to me that the thought and feeling of these poems, if expressed without any obscuring novelty of mode, are such as often to require the whole attention to apprehend and digest them; and are therefore of a kind to appeal only to the few. But to the already sufficiently arduous character of such poetry you seem to me to have added the difficulty of following *several* entirely novel and simultaneous experiments in versification and construction, together with an altogether unprecedented system of alliteration and compound

[120] See Ritz's excellent study *Robert Bridges and Gerard Hopkins 1863-1889.*

words;—any one of which novelties would be startling and productive of distraction from the poetic matter to be expressed.[121]

But no accumulation of like criticisms could shift Hopkins from his intuitive convictions. He conceded that his poetry was highly individual and "odd", and that this led to rejection by editors and the absence of a public. But until his work had been published and he could envisage an audience while he was actually composing, he could not see how he could become "more intelligible, smoother, and less singular".[122] He seemed to himself trapped in a fatal circle. In music he showed the same independence of current ideas. Untrained either in theory or in the playing of an instrument, he had tried to teach himself both.[123] His most original compositions spurned modulations, and seemed to himself to have "a character of their own which is neither that of modern major and minor music nor yet of the plain chant modes".[124]

Hopkins's service as a parish priest was limited to a total of only three years and four parishes—Oxford, Bedford Leigh, and Liverpool, with a brief spell in Glasgow. It came to an end with his tertianship (or second noviatiate) at Manresa from October 1881 to August 1882. During that time of refreshing he refrained from poetry, and indeed from all "wordly" matters, emerging spiritually stronger, but still unable to stand without strain the wear and fret of daily work or to take his place as a writer. He had, however, spent some of his tertianship writing parts of a valuable and penetrating commentary[125] on *The Spiritual Exercises of St Ignatius*, which will be frequently quoted in succeeding chapters.

---

[121] *Further Letters*, p. 352; cp. p. 353 at foot.   [122] *Letters*, p. 291.
[123] *Letters*, pp. 18, 30, 136; *Further Letters*, pp. 127, 238 etc.
[124] *Letters*, p. 305. See *J.P.*, pp. 457-9; and my own article "Gerard and Grace Hopkins", in *The Month*, n.s., xxxiii (Jun. 1965), pp. 347-50.   [125] Printed in *S.D.W.*, pp. 122-209.

After two years at Stonyhurst College, teaching Latin and Greek to students preparing for the external London B.A. degree, he was in January 1884 suddenly appointed Professor of Greek and Latin Literature in University College, Dublin, which had just been handed over to the Jesuits to run after an unfortunate early history.[126] So far from this being a crowning honour and filling Hopkins with confidence and the serenity of a well-merited post of distinction, this promotion was to bring him to a premature grave. Being an Englishman was no advantage in the Ireland of the 1880s. Most of Hopkins's students were external ones, who poured in volumes of examination scripts in six successive tidal waves every year. Hopkins marked these with the utmost scrupulous anxiety. The Society still retains stories of his rising in the middle of the night from a conscience-stricken bed to re-mark a script to which he felt he might have given too little or too much. The Royal University was indeed immersed in factional jealousies, and other Colleges complained that students at University College, Dublin, had an unfair advantage in being taught by the University examiners—an accusation which Hopkins was at great pains to falsify by not lecturing on forthcoming questions. His lectures were not always suited to his audience.

When Canon Dixon visited Dublin in 1893 after Hopkins's death, he talked to one of the Fathers who had known him well. Dixon wrote back to Bridges:

He, Father Cormac, had a great opinion of Gerard, without, I think, knowing of his genius. He spoke of him as a most delightful companion, and as excellent in his calling, and so on, intimating at the same time that there was something unusual about him: that he was fond of pursuing niceties to an extent that rather

[126] See *Letters*, pp. 316-7, n., and *A Page of Irish History: Story of University College Dublin 1883-1909*, compiled by Fathers of the Society of Jesus, Dublin 1930.

stood in the way of his general usefulness. As that he
dwelt on the niceties of the languages, in his classical
lectures, in a way that rather stopped the progress of
the classes. Also he was fond of taking up unusual
subjects for himself.[127]

Moreover, Hopkins was in his fortieth year when he
migrated to Ireland—a critical period in a man's life
when any latent conflicts are liable to assert themselves.
The state of mind to which he gave utterance in his sonnets and letters is discussed at some length in a later
chapter.[128] Father Devlin, speaking of the last year of
Hopkins's life, says: "Instead of being lifted to a closer
union in prayer, he found himself deteriorating not only
physically and mentally, but spiritually as well. . . ."[129]
His will, however, always turned him towards his high
goal, the pursuit of perfection, and he trod the path of
duty with determination, if with weakened steps. Devlin
adds: "Even if it is granted that they [Hopkins's trials]
were due to his own wilfulness, such noble wilfulness
seems to be always allowed for by God in the sanctifica-
tion of proudly courageous men like Hopkins."[130]

The retreat notes which Hopkins wrote the year before
his death reviewed his twenty years in the Society of
Jesus, and his "five wasted years" in Ireland:

I do not waver in my allegiance, I never have since
my conversion to the Church. The question is how I
advance the side I serve on. This may be inwardly or
outwardly. Outwardly I often think I am employed
to do what is of little or no use. . . . The Catholic
Church in Ireland and the Irish Province in it and our
College in that are greatly given over to a partly unlawful cause, promoted by partly unlawful means, and

[127] Dixon, quoted in James Sambrook, *A Poet Hidden: The Life of
Richard Watson Dixon 1833-1900*, (Athlone Press) 1962, pp. 96-7.
[128] See below, pp. 91 ff.
[129] *S.D.W.*, p. 218.   [130] *S.D.W.*, p. 219.

against my will my pains, laborious and distasteful, like prisoners made to serve the enemies' gunners, go to help on this cause. . . . I was continuing this train of thought this evening when I began to enter on that course of loathing and hopelessness which I have so often felt before, which made me fear madness and led me to give up the practice of meditation except, as now, in retreat and here it is again. I could therefore do no more than repeat *Justus es, Domine, et rectum judicium tuum* and the like, and then being tired I nodded and woke with a start. What is my wretched life? Five wasted years almost have passed in Ireland. I am ashamed of the little I have done, of my waste of time, although my helplessness and weakness is such that I could scarcely do otherwise. And yet the Wise Man warns us against excusing ourselves in that fashion. I cannot then be excused; but what is life without aim, without spur, without help? All my undertakings miscarry: I am like a straining eunuch. I wish then for death: yet if I died now I should die imperfect, no master of myself, and that is the worst failure of all. O my God, look down on me.[131]

After his second novitiate, as a Tertian, the Provincial had suggested that he might (in his spare time) write various books which Hopkins had told him he would like to produce.[132] But although his letters contain dozens of references to such projected works, each in turn seemed fated to frustration. In each case, Hopkins conceived a new idea with confidence and a desire that his "great and solid discovery"[133] should be published. Then came successive widenings of the field, as the scholar indulged his overpowering desire for completeness, reading more deeply and entering parallel areas of knowledge[134]—but at the same time postponing in-

131 *S.D.W.*, p. 261.   132 *Letters*, p. 150 (26 Sep. 1882).
133 *Letters*, p. 228.   134 *E.g.*, *Letters*, p. 241.

definitely the expenditure of exertion in writing down his theories and reducing them to a visible manuscript for the press. Every teacher and author is familiar with the effort needed to arrest at some point the comparatively pleasant process of study in order to begin the painful composition of an essay or lecture. Judging from the almost complete absence of any even partially finished manuscripts of books, Hopkins came to grief at this fatal transition stage.[135] As he sadly remarked to Bridges, "all my world is scaffolding".[136] His allusions to each project end in laments that he can make no headway, that he has insufficient energy to discharge the duties of his post with cheerfulness, let alone advance the honour of his Chair by distinguished publication.[137] Yet he turned to musical composition again, and persevered in his settings of poetry and the writing of fugues despite the criticisms of his unorthodox harmonies levelled by some of the professional musicians who saw them.[138]

Nevertheless, out of this prostration of mind and body, out of the "dryness of spirit" with which those in religious orders are all too familiar,[139] came poems and sonnets great in their intensity—the "Sonnets of Desolation" and other extended sonnets in which his poetic art reaches the heights.

It seems clear that his superiors encouraged Hopkins to seek the changes of environment which he himself realised that he needed[140]; as is indicated by his letters and the surviving account books in the Jesuit House at Lower Leeson Street, Dublin, Hopkins did move about

[135] We may note, however, that by 30 Jul. 1887 he claimed to have "written a good deal of my book on Metre": *Letters*, p. 256.
[136] *Letters*, p. 229.   [137] See, *e.g.*, *Letters*, p. 251.
[138] *Further Letters*, pp. 426 ff., and *Letters*, p. 248.
[139] See, *e.g.*, *The Letters of the late Father George Porter, S.J.*, New York 1891, esp. the early letters written while he was Master of Novices at Manresa when Hopkins was teaching rhetoric there.
[140] See, *e.g.*, *Letters*, p. 222, and letter to his father, 5 Jul. 1884, in *The Month*, n.s., xix (1958), pp. 265-6.

Ireland quite often in addition to paying short holiday visits to Scotland and Wales. He maintained an outward cheerfulness which, however, did not deceive such old friends as Francis de Paravicini, who met him in Dublin in 1888 and immediately on his return began to exert influence in the English Province of the Society to have him recalled to a more placid setting where he would be under less strain. And yet, although Fr Lahey's emphasis upon his "peace and happiness" in Ireland may be exaggerated, it is evident from his poems that Hopkins did enjoy many spells of comparative zest or tranquillity.[141]

If he had lived longer, he might have been transferred back to Stonyhurst or Manresa House to prepare English Catholics for university degrees, but before anything could be arranged, shortly after Low Sunday in 1889, he contracted typhoid fever, and died on 8 June, in his forty-fifth year. It is significant of the obscurity in which his poetic genius was concealed that in the account of his Dublin days written by "one of his most intimate friends",[142] though his musical compositions receive notice, his poetry is not so much as alluded to.

[141] Lahey, *Gerard Manley Hopkins*, pp. 140-7.
[142] *Letters and Notices*, xx (1890), p. 173.

CHAPTER II

WALES MOTHER OF MUSES

In December 1875, England was stirred by the graphic newspaper accounts of the disastrous wreck, twenty-seven miles off Harwich, of the emigrant ship the *Deutschland*, sailing from Germany to America. The terrible snowstorm in which the vessel was trapped on the lurking sandbank, the drowning of over sixty women, children, and men as the tide rose twenty feet to drive them from the decks into the freezing insecurity of the rigging, the culpable delay of more than twenty-four hours before her distress signals brought British rescue, the rifling of the bodies of the dead by the plundering boats which gathered afterwards—all these details were reported from eye-witness accounts or the evidence at the inquest. To the community at St Beuno's, on the far western edge of the island, safe from the cruel east gales, the news had an added significance, for among the drowned, their hands found linked together, were five Franciscan nuns who had been banished from their Westphalian convent by the edict of the Falk Laws.

> —On Saturday sailed from Bremen,
> American-outward-bound,
> Take settler and seamen, tell men with women,
> Two hundred souls in the round—
> O Father, not under thy feathers nor ever as guessing
> The goal was a shoal, of a fourth the doom to be
> drowned;
> Yet did the dark side of the bay of thy blessing
> Not vault them, the million of rounds of thy mercy not
> reeve even them in?

H D

Into the snows she sweeps,
Hurling the haven behind,
The Deutschland, on Sunday; and so the sky keeps,
For the infinite air is unkind,
And the sea flint-flake, black-backed in the regular
blow,
Sitting Eastnortheast, in cursed quarter, the wind;
Wiry and white-fiery and whirlwind-swivellèd snow
Spins to the widow-making unchilding unfathering deeps.

"The Wreck of the *Deutschland*" is very much more
than a tale of the sea, although most readers embarking
upon it for the first time might well start where Hopkins
himself began composing[1]—at Part II. Stanzas 11 to 17,
which carry the main story, are almost beyond praise.
After years of familiarity with them one still marvels at
the inspired invention of his cryptic words:

'Some find me a sword; some
The flange and the rail; flame,
Fang, or flood' goes Death on drum,
And storms bugle his fame.
But wé dream we are rooted in earth—Dust!
Flesh falls within sight of us, we, though our flower
the same,
Wave with the meadow, forget that there must
The sour scythe cringe, and the blear share come.[2]

Shirley's reference to the "poor crooked scythe and
spade" has here found a worthy successor, in which the
bitterness of death and the meanness of its sneaking implements are juxtaposed. The pace of the narrative
matches the blind-mad rush of the ship:

She drove in the dark to leeward,
She struck—not a reef or a rock
But the combs of a smother of sand: night drew her
Dead to the Kentish Knock. . . .[3]

[1] *Letters*, p. 44.
[2] "The Wreck of the *Deutschland*", St. 11.   [3] St. 14.

The speed is graphically halted by *smother*, followed by the sinister ambiguity of *dead*. The icy solidity of the waves catches us in the paradoxical "*cobbled* foam-*fleece*" (like sculptured tresses), and "*flint-flake*" sea. Even the wind strikes like water swirled into knots—but it, too, is an instrument of the Lord.[4] The compression and shattered structures of st. 17 harry us with their ruthless and precipitous candour:

> They fought with God's cold—
> And they could not and fell to the deck
> (Crushed them) or water (and drowned them) or rolled
> With the sea-romp over the wreck.
> Night roared, with the heart-break hearing a heart-broke rabble,
> The woman's wailing, the crying of child without check—

Expositions of the theme of "The Wreck of the *Deutschland*" are readily accessible.[5] Here we can only glance at the pervading and unifying imagery. Yet we should note that if the poem may seem hard to scan and construe, the inspired avoidance of hackneyed rhythms and phrases renders it so adult that alongside it other English verses about wrecks look like children's ballads, least comparable where they most invite comparison. One thinks, for example, of Longfellow's "Wreck of the *Hesperus*":

> She struck where the white and fleecy waves
>   Looked soft as carded wool,
> But the cruel rocks they gored her side
>   Like the horns of an angry bull.

Hopkins is no detached commentator: he has distilled himself into his narrative, his holy fears and tremblings,

---

[4] St. 16 ("the burl of the fountains of air"); cp. st. 13.
[5] See Bibliography (below, pp. 125-8) for studies by J. Keating and Elisabeth Schneider; also Notes in *Poems*, pp. 254-63.

his utter surrender, his devotion to his Church combining with his love of "rare-dear" Britain.

For Hopkins the wreck was a final culminating outside event, releasing the emotions and images which had been banking up throughout the seven silent years when the poetic channels had been closed off. The poem itself alludes to the suddenness with which the last barrier can be demolished and the divine current begin to flow. God can operate in either of two ways. The first is violent, symbolised here by the blinding lightning stroke[6]; the other is a gentle influence, a mild beam such as pulses out its stress from the beauty of the stars:

> lovely-asunder
> Starlight, wafting him out of it.[7]

These two modes of action are each supported by a whole group of fire images. Parallel with the "electrical horror" of the storm is the furnace fire of the smithy which can reduce resistant metal to malleable form[8]; there is the hot branding iron associated with the glorious death of the martyrs[9]; the warning flames of Hell[10]; the spiritual agony compared to a fire devouring the body from within[11]; the "dooms-day dazzle" of the Second Coming.[12] But the thunder-clouds can lift to show God, "Father and fondler of heart thou hast wrung", as the poet tells us in a stanza of haunting and deeply-felt beauty:

> For how to the heart's cheering
>   The down-dugged ground-hugged grey
> Hovers off, the jay-blue heavens appearing
>   Of pied and peeled May!
> Blue-beating and hoary-glow height; or night, still higher,
>   With belled fire and the moth-soft Milky Way. . . .[13]

[6] Sts. 2, 9, 27, 34.   [7] Sts. 5, 6.   [8] St. 10.   [9] St. 22.
[10] St. 3.   [11] St. 2.   [12] St. 34.   [13] St. 26.

The glimpse of vivid sky reminds him of the scintillating chequered blue on a jay's wing as it rises from a field.

Correlative with the "moth-soft Milky Way" are other temperate images of subdued light and fire—the "dappled-with-damson" display of the sunset[14]; the homely hearth-fire[15]; the life-beckoning warmth of Spring[16] or of dayspring[17]; a shower of falling gold.[18] When Christ is seen at the triumphant end of the poem as the "crimson-cresseted east",[19] we link this victorious dawn with the nun's radiating testimony to her faith, a "blown beacon of light",[20] burning the brighter on its rocky headland the harder the winds assail it.

Corresponding to these two groups of fire images, though less obvious, is the contrast between the haven and the high seas, between the boat tied to the sea wall and the ocean-ravaged *Deutschland*. God's providence rules paradoxically over the "unchilding unfathering deeps" just as fully as in the gentle tidal swell which lifts the moored ship (the Christian or priest), "at the wall fast". He is as much master of the placid ebb and flow as of the breakers with their "ruinous shock". And if we find the surge of ecstasy is followed by the wane, if the spiritual flood "crowds and it combs to the fall", if the believer's faith may drift to the very limits of its moorings, it is still secured to the granite pier. The vessel almost beached in low water beside the quay ("*under* the wall fast" as he originally wrote) is as much in His charge as the *Deutschland* caught on the smothering sandbank. Though our "motionable mind" may be as restless as the ocean and threaten us with shipwreck, God is its ground of being too, its containing wharf and coast-

---

[14] St. 5. [15] St. 35. [16] St. 10.
[17] St. 35. [18] Sts. 23, 34.
[19] The metaphor is from a blazing fire-basket being hoisted to guide a boat into harbour. Hopkins would know the supposed derivation of *cresset* from Fr. *croisette*, a little cross, as given, *e.g.*, in Ogilvie's *Imperial Dictionary*. [20] St. 29.

line.[21] God's complete mastery is the overriding theme
from the first stanza to the last[22]: but His domination,
whether asserted with might, or softly winning accept-
ance, is shown as only another aspect of His love. He is
both "a winter and warm".[23]

Coupled with the image of the moored vessel lifting
and lapsing with the tides, is the metaphor of the well:

> I steady as a water in a well, to a poise, to a pane,
> But roped with, always, all the way down from the
>   tall
>   Fells or flanks of the voel, a vein
> Of the gospel proffer, a pressure, a principle, Christ's
>   gift.[24]

The other imagery in this stanza discourages us, I think,
from imagining that the poet is comparing himself with
the holy well of St Winefred, whose level remained
miraculously constant under all conditions, a symbol
of Christ Himself rather than the fluctuating disciple.
His basic idea was of ordinary wells in a richly-watered
country, as the first form of the line would indicate:

> I steady, as the water in wells.

Fed from the hills, but enclosed within the protective
walls of the shaft, the level may fall as its supplies are
tapped, only to rise again in equipoise with the hidden
sponge waters around it, but seen from above it always
mirrors back the same panel of light.[25] "Roped" not only
"suggests the long silvery runnels down the mountain-

---

[21] Sts. 4, 32.

[22] See how "master", "mastery" echo through sts. 1, 10, 19, 21,
28, 32; along with the metaphors of God's Kingship which reinforce
these, sts. 10, 28, 32, 34, 35, etc.

[23] St. 9.

[24] St. 4.

[25] *J.P.*, p. 261 (Oct. 1874); see also p. 259 for Hopkins's association
of "panes" of sunlight and wells.

sides", as Professor Gardner finely remarks, but again emphasises the priest's bondage within grace.[26]

The poem is a spiritual autobiography as well as a graphic sea drama. The deliberate parallels between the ship in the grip of the storm:

> Into the snows she *sweeps*,
> *Hurling* the haven behind[27]

and the priest's experience in the Long Retreat—

> The swoon of a heart that the *sweep* and the *hurl* of thee trod
> Hard down with a horror of height[28]

—emphasise their identification in his mind.[29] The lightning, the fire of stress, the midriff and nerves astrain, can be experienced within the walls of the secluded chapel as painfully as among the "wind's burly and beat of endragonèd seas". In the willing heart the separating of good from evil may be as outwardly quiet as the softly-sifting hourglass, each grain of sand seen magnified and separate as it reaches the focus[30]; but with the half-penitent the jet of a tempest (of a demanding crisis) may be needed to winnow the shrouding husk from the wheat.[31]

There is just a hint of the theme which underlies "St. Alphonsus Rodriguez":

> The jading and jar of the cart,
> Time's tasking, it is fathers that asking for ease
> Of the sodden-with-its-sorrowing heart,
> Not danger, electrical horror.[32]

Martyrdom may be more spectacular, but the outwardly

---

[26] Cp. the moored ship in the same st., and George Herbert, "The Collar".

[27] St. 13; my italics.   [28] St. 2.

[29] Cp. sts. 2 and 3 with "Carrion Comfort", *Poems*, p. 99.

[30] St. 4.   [31] St. 31.   [32] St. 27.

uneventful life can produce a feeling of prostration which makes the lot of those "before-time-taken" seem almost enviable. While swift release came to the nuns, the poet remains pent in the cage of his body:

> Thou hast bound bones and veins in me, fastened
> me flesh,
> And after it almost unmade, what with dread,
> Thy doing.[33]

What a phrase that is, "the sodden-with-its-sorrowing heart"—Hopkins had already felt the choking pain which was to stifle almost everything in his last sonnets of desolation. But here his final vision is of the future empire of Christ:

> More brightening her, rare-dear Britain, as his
> reign rolls,
> Pride, rose, prince, hero of us, high-priest,
> Our hearts' charity's hearth's fire, our thoughts'
> chivalry's throng's Lord.[34]

Hopkins was never to compose such a grand symphony of words and emotions again.

"The Wreck of the *Deutschland*" was written in a rhythm which Hopkins thought of at first as "Miltonic": his earliest known use of the term "sprung rhythm" in writing is in the postscript to a letter written to Bridges over a year later, in 1877, after they had met to discuss rhythmic theories in London. In 1876 Hopkins was aware mainly of inverted feet, or "counterpoint" as he called it, by the use of which Milton had roughened his own verse. That Hopkins received chastening criticism for his own freedoms with metres and syntax we may deduce from the tone in which he introduces further poems in a letter home, "God's Grandeur" and "The Starlight Night"—

[33] *Ibid.* Cp. Marvell, "A Dialogue between the Soul and the Body", st. 1.
[34] St. 35.

two sonnets I wrote in a freak the other day. . . . They are not so very queer, but have a few metrical effects, mostly after Milton, as in his—

"Light from above, from the fountain of light—"

. . . These rhythms are not commonly understood but do what nothing else can in their contexts.[35]

His family found "God's Grandeur" opening with a line containing what the poet called "double counterpoint" —reversed rhythm in two successive feet:

The world is charged with the grandeur of God. . . .

But we must reserve the complications of sprung rhythm for a separate chapter.[36]

The remarkable twenty months which elapsed between Hopkins's undertaking a poem on the wreck of the *Deutschland* and his leaving Wales in October 1877 saw the production of what was to be about one third of his mature and finished poetry. Moreover, the poems of this period have a spontaneity about them which was seldom to return to him in later times. Not that he was, "on a pastoral forehead of Wales", in truth as fully "at rest" as he had suggested in his great poem.[37] It is not without significance that "Penmaen Pool", written the same year as "The Wreck of the *Deutschland*", begins "Who long for rest . . .", and closes with a reference to those who "pine for peace".

His letters from Wales allude again and again to the severity of his course of study in theology, which left little time and no energy for wider reading. In a sermon preached in March 1877 he generalised from his own

---

[35] *Further Letters*, p. 144. See Hopkins had apologetically used the word "freak" of a rhyme in "Penmaen Pool" a few months before: *op. cit.*, p. 141.

[36] "Sprung rhythm" is discussed below, pp. 100-11.

[37] "The Wreck of the *Deutschland*", st. 24.

feeling of exhaustion: "if tired we complain as if no
sleep or rest would ever refresh us; . . . I speak of what
I know in myself."[38] He was in fact worried on various
scores during his years at St Beuno's; and the Provincial
decided to cut them short. The comparative freshness of
his lyric vein despite all this is proof of his faith and of
his glowing affection for the Welsh scenes around him,
"more charming and touching than ever: in its way
there can hardly be in the world anything to beat the
Vale of Clwyd".[39] Nevertheless, excluding the com-
missioned "Silver Jubilee", in its English, Welsh, and
Latin versions, out of the eleven most important poems
of his Welsh period, only three show a full escape from
sadness: "The Starlight Night", "Pied Beauty" and
"Hurrahing in Harvest", though even with the last his
heart only "half hurls earth for him off under his feet."[40]

That the "Starlight Night" should appear untroubled
was not due to a spell of serenity. It was composed on
the same day as a disturbed reply to Bridges: in fact one
autograph, containing many early readings, is written
on the back of a sheet on which he had struggled to find
the best ways in which to correct his friend's misappre-
hensions about such things as the censoring of his letters.
He tells of "a very serious examination" in moral theology to take place that week, a prospect which might well
have driven poetry from his mind.[41] But at this stage in
his life a surge of inspiration could sweep away every
care in the all-absorbing process of composition.

Hopkins shared with George Herbert a fascination for
the stars. From his earliest poems, through the jottings

---

[38] *Letters*, pp. 30-3; *Further Letters*, pp. 131-4, 143, 144, 146;
S.D.W., p. 230; cp. *J.P.*, p. 258.

[39] *Further Letters*, p. 137.

[40] The parallel with Plato's *Phaedrus* 249 C-D is striking: the true
philosopher, says Plato, gazing upon the beauty of the world, re-
collects the heavenly beauty of which it is a lesser copy. He feels the
wings of his soul growing, and yearns to soar into flight, but cannot.

[41] *Letters*, pp. 31-2.

in his undergraduate diaries, his Latin verse, right down
to his meditations and poems in Dublin (such as "Spelt
from Sibyl's Leaves" and "That Nature is a Heraclitean
Fire") scores of allusions to the heavenly bodies can be
found. He had not always read the stars with the eye of
faith as he does in "The Starlight Night". In the Lent of
1866, just before his conversion, he had written in a vein
reminiscent of Tennyson's *In Memoriam*:

> Night to a myriad worlds gives birth,
> Yet like a lighted empty hall
> Where stands no host at door or hearth
> Vacant creation's lamps appal.[42]

But in this poem there is direct reminiscence of George
Herbert rather than Hopkins's own contemporary
Tennyson:

> Gold thou mayst safely touch; but if it stick
> Unto thy hands, it woundeth to the quick. . . .
>
> Take starres for money; starres not to be told
> By any art, yet to be purchased.[43]

Another immediate influence can be traced through the
alliteration and echoes. Welsh poetry abounded with
recurring chimes of consonants and internal rhymes, and
Hopkins frequently juggled his ideas and words around
until he had approximated as closely as he could to this
device. In the case of "The Starlight Night" we have
five autograph drafts all different, two of them with foot-

---

[42] *Poems*, p. 32. Cp. *S.D.W.*, p. 262: "It is as if one were dazzled by
a spark or star in the dark, seeing it but not seeing by it: we want a
light shed on our way and a happiness spread over our life" (1888).

[43] George Herbert, "The Church Porch", ll. 167-8, 171-2. Note,
too, the odd parallel of "gold . . . quick" with "quickgold"; cp. also
(1) the astronomer in "Herbert's Vanity I" who surveys the spheres
"as if he had design'd/To make a purchase there", and (2) "Misery",
l. 52; "No, not to purchase the whole pack of starres."

note afterthoughts; one transcript corrected by Hopkins (but not representing his final thoughts even so); and another transcript which Bridges made in August 1884 from the ultimately satisfying version. The fourth line originally ran:

> Look, the elf-rings! look at the out-round earnest eyes!

Rhythmically the line illustrated his remark to Bridges that he himself went further than Bridges did in the way of irregularity.[44] Between 3 March (when he copied it for his mother) and 3 April (when he sent it to Bridges) he had tried changing "earnest" to "eager", and then completely remodelled the line:

> The dim woods quick with diamond wells; the elf-eyes!

He had now added sparkle and mystery to the thought, besides approximating towards the intricate compound alliteration which figured in Welsh poetry—*cynghanedd*. Here we have two consonants repeated in the same order: *dim, diam*—. Having satisfied himself with both the imagery and the vocal ingredients of the line, Hopkins restlessly rearranged the principal words in eight different ways. But the success of the line became assured when he remembered a current dialect word for a pit or quarry—*delf*—and with its musical aid produced something similar to the Welsh *cynghanedd sain*. By this interesting pattern the line is divided into three sections (in Hopkins's example very uneven divisions), of which the first two rhyme and the last two alliterate:

> Down in dim woods the diamond *delves*!/the *elves'*/eyes!

Behind the sestet, but seldom recognised, lurk suggestions from the Parable of the Foolish Virgins, waiting in the night for the bridegroom to return, their unreplenished oil lamps fluttering out into blackness. They

[44] *Letters*, p. 38.

too were told to go and *buy*, but when they returned the spouse had come home with his bride (the Church), and the door was shut.[45]

"No one is ever so poor", wrote Hopkins in a sententious mood, "that he is not . . . owner of the skies and stars and everything wild that is to be found on the earth."[46] Although his love of flowers and the blossoming trees is obvious from the *Journals*, in poetry from the beginning he expressed a special feeling of affinity with the weeds growing where and as they pleased. This was not a reaction to the discipline of serving God, but it certainly did reflect his rebuttal of the idea that there was only one respectable shape of conduct, whether in poetry, civil life, or his Church. His conviction that God delights in things that are different meant that this creed of inscaped and original personalities was not in conflict with his devotion. With the weeds Hopkins associated in his affection trees, provided they had not been "improved" by hewing and clipping. "Binsey Poplars" brings together the sun-quenching poplars with the "wind-wandering weed-winding bank" on which they had been growing. His drawings were more often of tangled banks than of the more respectable flowers.

At a later stage, when the hard streets of Liverpool had almost destroyed his Muse, the wild abandon of the brae and its banks at Inversnaid brought a flow of free lyricism absent from all his surrounding verse. And here in Wales we find asserted with a charming lack of polemics God's refusal to show exclusive favour to the carefully trimmed character.

Both "Spring" and "Pied Beauty" reject any indentification of saintliness with Victorian respectability. The same belief that it was often a virtue to be different produced the rebellious trochaic opening to "Spring", the delightful "curtal sonnet" shape of "Pied Beauty", as

---

[45] Mt. xxv. 1-13; cp. Dan. xii. 3.
[46] *Further Letters*, p. 111.

well as the unconventional distribution of praise to be found in both these poems.

> Nothing is so beautiful as Spring—
> When weeds . . . .

We pause to take the shock of such a line in an age when Tennyson and others identified weeds with sin.[47] Hopkins recognises in spring a reminder of the Garden of Eden—no flat and symmetrical formal garden—a sort of Versailles—such as some had envisaged it, but a place almost free from set laws. "There it lies, the bliss of that Paradise, the native virtue of that green garden, the easy constitution of that first commonwealth of God", he declared in a sermon on the earthly paradise.[48]

> Nothing is so beautiful as Spring—
> When weeds, in wheels, shoot long and lovely and lush.

The whole sonnet reverberates with freedom. It is not only the lambs who have "fair their fling". Everything is unconfined: the tiny thrush's eggs expand for him into little heavens of ecstasy; the note of the thrush strikes out boldly over the countryside, resonating among the tree trunks; as he gazes up from beneath the orchard trees, their branches, stretching infinitely wide, seem to waver under the spill of a waterfall-sky, for the azure itself is cascading on to the earth. Everything is fluid instead of set. But only Christ can preserve this happy Eden. Sin can make the flow of joy clog or cloy; it can cloud over and freeze the liquid heavens; it can sour and clot the juice. The Mayday of a youthful world can turn to a Christless winter.

Even the Welsh landscape around St Beuno's, though

---

[47] *E.g.*, the dedication of "The Palace of Art": "A sinful soul possess'd of many gifts,/A spacious garden full of flowering weeds"; cp. "Two Voices", l. 142, or "Lovers' Tale", l. 525.

[48] *S.D.W.*, p. 60.

deeply satisfying, had not escaped the imprint of the age. In "The Sea and the Skylark", dated Rhyl, May 1877, Hopkins finds the upstart seaside holiday resort of Rhyl —"this shallow and frail town"—a symbol of "our sordid turbid time".[49] Rhyl lay five miles away from their College, where the waters of his beloved River Elwy, having joined the Clwyd, became sluggish in the Rhuddlan Marsh, which bounded the town on the west. Hopkins associates the town with the slimy marsh, like the primeval mud from which man was first created by God to become the crown of nature. Hopkins did not share the confidence in human progress which some of his contemporaries, such as Herbert Spencer and Carlyle, preached so insistently. "Find Mankind where thou wilt," Carlyle had written, "thou findest it in living movement, in progress faster or slower: the Phoenix soars aloft, hovers with outstretched wings, filling Earth with her music; or, as now, she sinks, and with spheral swan-song immolates herself in flame, that she may soar the higher and sing the clearer."[50] But Hopkins, listening to the lark in its soaring, heard, not the voice of progress, but a song which brought back for him the lost "cheer and charm" of the earthly Paradise. Behind the poem lie Hopkins's thoughts on the current theories of evolution. Shortly before reaching St Beuno's he had, for instance, read the presidential address to the British Association of John Tyndall, a man at whose door W. B. Yeats laid his own loss of faith. It was full of a vague and diffuse Darwinism; looking "back to an obscure origin, he looks forward with the same content to an obscure future".[51]

[49] Fr A. Thomas, s.j., tells me that the Beadle's Journal at St Beuno's records: "9 May, 1877: Mr G. Hopkins went to Rhyl for the good of his health." He returned on 14 May.

[50] *Sartor Resartus*, Book III, ch. 7. Hopkins, writing to Dixon about Carlyle, declared (*Correspondence*, p. 59): "I hate his principles, I burn most that he worships and worship most that he burns."

[51] To his mother, 20 Sep. 1874, *Further Letters*, pp. 127-8.

The first line in its inelegance mirrors the bewildering impact of the two sounds upon him:

> On ear and ear *two* noises *too* old *to* end
> Trench—

sluicing furrows in his hearing with their violence. From one side comes the ramping of the tide, from the other the pelting song of the lark, rash as a rain-storm, both intense enough to be described as *noises* rather than *sounds*. Like the wild clatter of Tennyson's New Year bells, they seem to "ring right out" this "shallow and frail town".[52]

Another sonnet, "The Caged Skylark", written that same year, centres around the bird already famous through the odes of Wordsworth and Shelley. But his "Windhover" raised to a position of rival prominence a bird scarcely mentioned by previous poets. The volume of commentary which this sonnet has produced is evidence of its continuing fascination, but we have room here only for a consideration of the reason why it was dedicated to Christ.

"The Windhover" was originally written on 30 May 1877. Hopkins did not add to the title until six and a half years later, between December 1883 and March 1884. He was then revising a volume of transcripts of his poems which Bridges had beautifully copied out in order to circulate among his friends—an album which later passed into Hopkins's own possession and is now known as Ms. B.[53] Why did Hopkins add "to Christ our Lord"? Fr W. A. M. Peters is convinced that there is only one explanation, namely that it was the best thing he ever wrote.[54] Peters interprets the flames of infinitely greater beauty in the sestet as referring to the windhover "dis-

---

[52] Cp. "The Wreck of the *Deutschland*", st. 19 ("rash smart sloggering brine").

[53] For the history of Ms. B, see *Poems*, p. 232.

[54] Peters, *Gerard Manley Hopkins*, pp. 85-6; cp. *Letters*, p. 85.

playing all its majestic splendours in its flight" compared
with its lesser glory when "just hanging on the wing".
A study of the original draft of the poem induces me to
offer a different explanation. Headed simply "The
Windhover", the poem ran:

> I caught this morning morning's minion, king
>   Of daylight's dauphin, dapple-dawn-drawn
>   Falcon . . . .

It will be seen that the falcon shares our attention with
a more important figure, the "king of daylight". The
bird is only the minion of morning. Hopkins's Welsh
studies would have reminded him of the word from
which "minion" was in those days commonly derived—
the Welsh *main*, "small", with its related *mwyn*, "tender,
gentle".[55] The subordinate note in "minion" is almost
inescapable. Whereas the "king" is assigned a position
of isolated rhythmic strength at the end of the first line,
the windhover is no more than dauphin. Though he may
conquer the wind, he himself is drawn out by the dawn.
In this version the sonnet prepared the reader more
adequately for the sestet, in which the poet turns from
the prince to the reigning Monarch Himself. The familiar
scriptural concept of Christ as the "dayspring" or sunrise, "the Sun of righteousness", had formed the climax
to his recently finished "Wreck of the *Deutschland*". The
poet saw the dappled beauty of physical dawn and sunset as displaying the mysterious wonder of God Himself.[56]
In the sestet of this sonnet he contrasts the flashing
plumage and flaming courage of the brute bird with the
billion times greater radiance of the sunrise and the
King of Daylight.

[55] Cp. Ogilvie's *Imperial Dictionary*, 2 vols., first published in 1850.
I quote always from my own copy of the edn. published in 1859.
[56] See "The Wreck of the *Deutschland*", sts. 5, 35, etc. Note how
many words from the last stanza are echoed in this sonnet: *king,
pride, rolls, heart, hearth's fire, chivalry.*

> Brute beauty and valour and act, oh, air, pride, plume, here
> Buckle! AND the fire that breaks from thee then, a billion
> Times told lovelier, more dangerous, O my chevalier!

There has been long debate as to whether the poet can be imagined as speaking to Christ rather than to the kestrel or his own heart. If to the kestrel, then the language is surely extravagant—"a billion Times told lovelier". Honour may certainly be flashed off even such physical exploits, but the poet's stir of enthusiasm can be better paralleled by "Hurrahing in Harvest" written that same year. The upsurge of joy there which made him feel that he could hurl earth away like a soaring bird was not due to the stately floating of silk-sack clouds, but to the inrushing feeling that these were revelations of God Himself—that the hills *were* "his world-wielding shoulder Majestic!" Just as Christ is reborn to the world through the witness of one brave martyr,[57] so the grandeur of God will flame out, beautiful and awe-inspiring, from the imperfect "perfection" of one of His creatures. Their duller glory can be converted into a divine irradiance when such a sight "meets" a human heart in a receptive and perceptive mood.[58] In two other sonnets written that same month, Hopkins opens with a general description in octave and early sestet, then suddenly ends in a direct address to Christ or God. "Spring" runs on through its lush description of thrush-eggs and pear-blossom, but the last four lines are a prayer:

> Have, get, before it cloy,
> Before it cloud, Christ, lord . . .

[57] "The Wreck of the *Deutschland*", sts. 30, 34.
[58] See "The Wreck of the *Deutschland*", st. 5, l. 8, and "Hurrahing in Harvest", l. 12.

His sonnet "In the Valley of the Elwy", composed exactly a week before "The Windhover", also climaxes in an address to "God, lover of souls . . .". The transition here from kestrel to Christ is not abrupt or incongruous. Christ is addressed as "my chevalier", as though, like the bird, he rode the air. The image of Christ as a hawk or eagle is implicit in "The Wreck of the *Deutschland*", sts. 2, 3, where the poet compares himself to a dove, remembering

> The swoon of a heart that the swoop and the
>   hurl of thee trod
> Hard down with a horror of height.[59]

The phrase "king of daylight's dauphin" survived the revision of 1879,[60] but in 1884 the poet must have noticed the lurking ambiguity. Was the falcon "the king of the dauphin of daylight" or "the dauphin of the king of daylight"? The word *king* was part of the basic rhyme-pattern of the octave (*wing*, *swing*, *thing*) and to change it would cripple both sense and sound. He hit upon a brilliant and bold emendation:

> king-
>   dom of daylight's dauphin . . .

—rhythmically more exciting, yet retaining the central imagery and rhymes. But the King himself was gone. So to prevent misunderstanding he put the King into the very title of the poem: "to Christ our Lord". This surely is the explanation of the manuscript change—the sonnet is addressed to the King himself, whose splendour transcends the utmost which His creation can offer.

Yet how varied and attractive these lesser, earthly sights can be is set out in his artistically shortened sonnet, "Pied Beauty". Hopkins praises God for brindled

---

[59] In 1884 Hopkins altered "swoop" to "sweep", bringing the image more into line with the ship swept and hurled in God's snowstorm (st. 13).   [60] *Letters*, p. 85.

cows and blacksmith's anvils as well as for the so-called poetic objects around him. He whose beauty is past change is recognised as fathering forth the slow and the sour, the shade as well as the light. Pleasant little echoes ripple and lap through the poem—*dappled, couple, stipple, tackle, fickle, freckled, adazzle. Fold* may be taken two ways —of a sheepfold and its associated meadows, or the folds in the ground: Hopkins had observed how "hills, just fleeced with grain or other green growth, by their dips and waves foreshortened here and there and so differenced in brightness and opacity the green on them, with delicate effect".[61]

All Hopkins's senses were preternaturally responsive— hearing, touch, taste, sight. Yet no one could be further from the voluptuousness of an Oscar Wilde. If "Pied Beauty" sparkles with light and colour, "The Lantern out of Doors" presents us with an Egyptian darkness which can be felt. A man's life is compared to a lantern pulsing out beams of light against the morbid pressure of the "much-thick and marsh air". Deeper and deeper into the darkness wades the vital lamp, winding along an eddying path, until the devouring distance swamps it into symbolic death. We recall a later poem, "That Nature is a Heraclitean Fire", where the imagery has been intensified: Man's life and the memory of it seem there only a momentary spark struck from a flint, while the darkness of death has become primeval chaos, a bottomless abyss which no fire could warm:

> Both are in an unfathomable, all is in an
> enormous dark
> Drowned.[62]

In yet another sonnet the poet wakens to "feel the fell of dark" pressing upon him like a leaden pall.[63]

"The Lantern", as it was originally called, commemorates the friends whom he had helped or admired,

[61] *J.P.*, p. 133.   [62] *Poems*, p. 105.   [63] *Poems*, p. 101.

but had lost either through death[64] or through separating distance. The imagery of this sonnet, dated simply "1877", seems to me to issue out of autumn, when damp fogs spread over the Clwyd Valley,[65] and the mood itself would accord with his impending severance from his fellow theologians at St Beuno's in October 1877, with many of whom he had spent three crucial years:

> Death or distance soon consumes them: wind
> What most I may eye after.

Bridges objected to the notion of "eyes winding", though indeed they had been recognised as "bending" since classical times.[66] While Hopkins was driven into a lamely mathematical defence where none was really called for,[67] he asserted his independence within a few months of this correspondence by using a still bolder metaphor for the beam between eye and flame in "The Candle Indoors", and by pointedly renaming his earlier sonnet "The Lantern out of Doors", to establish the two as companion pieces.[68]

But separating the two sonnets lay more than a year of varied occupations for the newly ordained priest—a few months at Chesterfield, then at Stonyhurst, a spell at London's famous Farm Street Church, and finally parish work at Oxford. "The Lantern" was perhaps the last poem written at St Beuno's: it seems to me to foreshadow the increasing seriousness in his lyrics from this point onwards. They seldom thereafter recaptured the exuberance of the sonnets written in Wales.

One exception is to be found in a poem which blossomed out of the following spring, the "May Magni-

---

[64] See *J.P.*, pp. 219, 234, 243, 260; *Further Letters*, pp. 128, 147-8.
[65] *J.P.*, pp. 260-1; see MacKenzie, "Gerard and Grace Hopkins", p. 348.   [66] Cp. Ovid, *Met.*, viii. 696 ("flexere oculos").
[67] *Letters*, pp. 66-7.
[68] For a possible interpretation of this difficult image, see below, p. 73.

ficat".[69] Written in exquisite simplicity mingled with a virtuoso's disregard for conventions, it was intended for anonymous display on the statue of the Blessed Virgin at Stonyhurst. But what we recognise as sprung rhythm must have sounded to the Rector like missing syllables:

> Her feasts follow reason,
> Dated due to season—
>
> Candlemas, Lady Day;
> But the Lady Month, May, . . .

Its ellipses or ambiguities of syntax[70] would be as perplexing as his "misuse" of words,[71] and the rhyming of *breasted* with *nest-hid*.[72] At any rate, the work of others was preferred, and the "May Magnificat" was banished. Another official voice had informed Hopkins that his poetry was of dubious service to the Church.[73]

Looking back through a century upon an age sometimes surprisingly remote from ours in gait, garb, and sympathies, we can only regret that so few could be found to encourage a poet who was able to end a poem on the Virgin Mary with these spirited stanzas:

> When drop-of-blood-and-foam-dapple
> Bloom lights the orchard-apple
>   And thicket and thorp are merry
>   With silver-surfèd cherry
>
> And azuring-over greybell makes
> Wood banks and brakes wash wet like lakes
>   And magic cuckoocall
>   Caps, clears, and clinches all—

[69] May 1878: *Poems*, p. 76.

[70] *E.g.*, in the last stanza. In the original version, ll. 11-12 were more direct: "Is it opportunest,/Finding flowers the soonest?"

[71] Such as, *sizing*, l. 25.

[72] In l. 20; later changed to *nested*.

[73] Cp. Prof. C. C. Abbott's conjecture that the poem was not solemn enough: *Letters*, p. 77, n. 2. See also Ritz, *Le Poète Gérard Manley Hopkins*, pp. 462-4.

> This ecstasy all through mothering earth
> Tells Mary her mirth till Christ's birth
>   To remember and exultation
>   In God who was her salvation.

Though during a much later appointment at Stonyhurst Hopkins had a May poem accepted, he felt that he had achieved this partly through "a compromise with popular taste".[74] That he made some effort even in 1878 both to please and to instruct is shown by an important composition to which we must now turn back: "The Loss of the *Eurydice*".

It is inevitable that "The Loss of the *Eurydice*" should be compared with "The Wreck of the *Deutschland*". Both were "occasional poems", stimulated into being by a disaster at sea. Both moved the priest profoundly enough to break a period in which he had written nothing, though on the second occasion the Museless time had been only seven months, not seven years. Both were unsuccessfully submitted to *The Month* for publication, becoming what Hopkins facetiously called his "two almost famous Rejected Addresses".[75]

There can be no doubt that Hopkins himself set out to avoid some of the stumbling-blocks which "The Wreck of the *Deutschland*" had encountered. Bridges had at first refused to labour through the length of the earlier poem a second time, and complained moreover that there was too much homily and insufficient narrative. The Jesuit editors had jibbed at the metrical marks upon which the poet had insisted. Hopkins therefore made "The Loss of the *Eurydice*" shorter, simpler, more directly concerned with the events (until the last nine stanzas), and void of all stress marks. His care won him partial success: the reactions of his two poet friends were favourable. Bridges, usually thrifty of praise, em-

---

[74] "The Blessed Virgin compared to the Air we Breathe", May 1883, *Poems*, p. 93; *Letters*, p. 179.   [75] *Letters*, p. 59.

barrassed the priest with his compliments, and while
Canon Dixon acknowledged that "The Wreck of the
Deutschland" was enormously powerful, he obviously pre-
ferred the later poem: "The Eurydice no one could read
without the deepest and most ennobling emotion."[76]
The author himself conceded that "The Loss of the
Eurydice" might show more mastery both in its art and
the handling of the sprung rhythm, but he realised, as
all subsequent critics must, that "the best lines in the
Deutschland are better than the best in the other".[77]

The two subjects are only superficially alike. The
passengers in the *Deutschland*, a foreign ship, were subjected to long-drawn agonies in the heartless fury of a
mid-winter storm. But the *Eurydice*, a Royal Naval training vessel, was triumphantly within sight of land after a
six-month voyage, racing confidently home on a blue
March day under full canvas, when a sudden blast of
wind and snow capsized her, sending her to the bottom
with the loss of over three hundred boys and men. Two
boys alone escaped. Only one comparable disaster could
be recalled in the annals of the British Navy.[78]

"The Loss of the *Eurydice*" is almost as much a patriotic
poem as a religious one. Hopkins proudly adopts the
current description of British sailors and their ships as
"hearts of oak", and in a vivid metaphor he pictures them
as sturdy trees struck down and buried in the cleaving
earth by a single lightning flash, within peaceful sound
of the sheepbells on the headlong slopes of the coast.

His emphasis is upon the way in which both ship and
men were caught unawares, no time for death-hour
repentance. The abruptness of the opening mirrors the
swiftness of the disaster:

---

[76] *Letters*, p. 52; *Correspondence*, p. 32.   [77] *Letters*, p. 119.
[78] For contemporary reports and comments, assembled by Fr
Norman Weyand, s.j., and for an exhaustive though somewhat unequal analysis of the poem by Fr Youree Watson, s.j., see *Immortal
Diamond*, edd. Weyand and Schoder, pp. 375-92 and 307-32.

The Eurydice—it concerned thee, O Lord:
Three hundred souls, O alas! on board,
   Some asleep unawakened, all un-
Warned, eleven fathoms fallen

Where she foundered! One stroke
Felled and furled them, the hearts of oak!
   And flockbells off the aerial
Downs' forefalls beat to the burial.[79]

The poem is curiously uneven. Hopkins insisted upon trying out a Welsh type of linked rhyme in which he ignored the junctures created by word-ends, and even by line-ends, in order to rhyme, e.g., *coast or M-* [*ark*] with *snowstorm*.[80] Whatever technical virtuosity this displays, it cannot wholly banish the comic associations which even plain double rhymes have acquired through Thomas Hood and W. S. Gilbert. Moreover, mispronunciation is involved, not merely with *foot he/ . . .duty/* (an instance which Hopkins noticed and changed), but with *all un-/ . . .fallen/*; *England/ . . . mingle? and/*; *wrecked her? he C-/ . . . electric/* (where the *h* of *he* has to be dropped, Cockney-fashion). In l. 39 *portholes* must become *portals* if it is to chime with *mortals*. I cannot help feeling that the deep solemnity of the final lines is threatened by the rhyme:

    Not that hell knows redeeming,
    But for souls sunk in seeming
       Fresh, till doomfire burn all,
    Prayer shall fetch pity eternal.

[79] Sts. 1, 2. Bridges (*Letters*, p. 52) challenged *furled*, and *bole* (l. 16), which continues the same figure. The "forefalls" of the "aerial downs" refers in Hampshire dialect to the steep valleys pitching down to the sea.

[80] See *Letters*, p. 48. For 19th-cent. Welsh equivalents, see W. H. Gardner, *Gerard Manley Hopkins*, II. 153. In "These Old Men", Geoffrey Tillotson more recently rhymed *first* with . . . *worse*". *T/ime*, ignoring a full stop. Hopkins wanted 'rigidly good' rhymes. *Letters*, p. 44.

Hopkins later told his brother Everard that his own
"run-over rhymes were experimental, perhaps a mistake",[81] and he confessed to Bridges: "I am sure I have
gone far enough in oddities and running rhymes . . . into
the next line."[82]

But the poem more than repairs such superficial
blemishes by the vigour of its descriptions,[83] and by the
inventiveness of its poetic compounds: *champ-white*, *wolf-
snow*, *hailropes*, *baldbright*, *wildworth* (beautifully glossed
by Fr Schoder as "virtue or character all about us, as
though springing up wild in the soil of human nature".)
Two coinages were sacrificed during revisions—*mortholes*,
used for the fatal open ports into which the sea roared as
the vessel heeled over, and *grimstones*, a word which might
have come from *Beowulf* rather than from the name of a
respectable Jesuit colleague.[84]

"The Loss of the *Eurydice*" is imbued with the same
sort of affection which Hopkins developed as teacher and
parish-priest for the fine young lads under his charge, as
we find in a set of poems: "The Bugler's First Communion"—the young soldier from the Cowley Barracks,

[81] *Poems*, p. 243 n.

[82] *Letters*, p. 250. In the original *Rejected Addresses*, by H. & J.
Smith, which saw 18 edns, 1812-33, and with which Hopkins amus-
ingly compares (*Letters*, p. 59) his two "wrecks", these rhymes are
successfully used to achieve bathos. See *Punch's Apotheosis*, e.g.: *be an
actor in/ . . . manufacturing/; immaculate/ . . . knack o' late/; Goneril/ . . .
upon her heel*. Presumably because he takes *seeming/Fresh* as adjective
and noun, Fr Schoder (*Immortal Diamond*, edd. Weyand and Schoder,
p. 205) glosses *Fresh* "flood, tide, rush of new water in a river or sea".
But the first version in Ms. A ran: "But lives rise yet sunk in seeming,
And fresh, till doomfire . . .". Hence *seeming* is really a noun, and
Fresh is an adjective qualifying *Prayer*: for souls seemingly sunk,
fresh prayer will go on ascending until the day of judgement pro-
nounces final verdict.

[83] *E.g.*, ll. 21-36, 77-84.

[84] Though it is a surname, derived from a place-name, its elements
may still be *grim* and *stone*. Hopkins replaced the word with *heaven-
gravel*. See *Letters*, pp. 53-4, and Elisabeth Schneider in *M.L.N.*,
LXV (1950), p. 310.

eagerly attending his first mass; "The Handsome Heart"
—a tribute to the keen youngster who assisted him when
he was hard-pressed in the Oxford parish through his
Superior's illness; "Brothers"—about the older schoolboy at Mount St Mary's who submerged his own interests in those of his unabashed brother Jack.[85] His admiration of their fine traits of body and mind, and his
longing to see them redeemed and preserved, fill the last
section of "The Loss of the *Eurydice*" and the first stanza
of "Morning, Midday, and Evening Sacrifice":

> The dappled die-away
> Cheek and the wimpled lip,
> The gold-wisp, the airy-grey
> Eye, all in fellowship—
> This, all this beauty blooming,
> This, all this freshness fuming,
> Give God while worth consuming.[86]

[85] *Poems*, pp. 81-3, 87.   [86] *Poems*, p. 84.

CHAPTER III

FROM OXFORD TO LANCASHIRE

Hopkins's return to Oxford in the last month or so of 1878, as assistant parish priest at St Aloysius, brought him little satisfaction. The city was rapidly changing, and between the Presbytery (close to St Giles) and the river a crowd of mean streets and ugly brick houses had sprung up since his Balliol days, separating the dignified grey of the Colleges from the green of the meadows which used to shoulder it.[1] The ambivalence of his bearing towards the city of Oxford is displayed in his well-known sonnet, "Duns Scotus's Oxford".[2] He seems alternately allured and pained. The city was "cuckoo-echoing"[3] but also "bell-swarmèd". As an undergraduate in 1865 he had written of Oxford's "towers musical",[4] but to the priest they now sounded the summons to a heretical worship. "Religion, you know", he told Baillie when writing about his distrust of Oxford, "enters very deep; in reality it is the deepest impression I have in speaking to people, that they are or that they are not of my religion."[5] The poem pits "lark-charmèd"

---

[1] *Letters*, p. 20. Those who love Oxford and its history may compare *Webster's Oxford Directory* (1869), just after Hopkins went down, with *The Times Oxford City and Suburban Directory* (1876). Such streets as Jericho St., Juxon St., Albert St., Cardigan St., Kingston Rd., and St. John's Rd. had spread from almost nothing in the interval. They were inhabited by tradesmen and artisans.

[2] *Poems*, p. 79.

[3] Refs. in Hopkins's poems, journals and letters confirm his delight in the cuckoo: *Poems*, p. 78 ("magic cuckoocall"); *J.P.*, p. 232 (cp. *J.P.*, pp. 138, 165, 190, 191, 208), and *Letters*, pp. 145-6.

[4] *Poems*, p. 21.   [5] *Further Letters*, p. 245.

and "river-rounded" against "rook-racked". Outwardly
he seems perturbed mainly by the brickish suburbia
which the city had accreted in the previous fifty years,
but in order to find an image of town and university
which he could wholly rest upon, he went back to the
thirteenth century, far into Catholic times, when Duns
Scotus taught and meditated within the walls or beside
the stealing weed-fringed rivers. The reference in the
last tercet is no pious afterthought, but contrasts the soul-
satisfying doctrines of Duns Scotus, whom Hopkins had
come to love, with the Greek and Latin philosophers and
dramatists on whom the classical education of the Oxford
undergraduates continued to depend.

> Yet ah! this air I gather and I release
> He lived on; these weeds and waters, these
>   walls are what
> He haunted who of all men most sways my
>   spirits to peace;
> Of realty the rarest-veinèd unraveller; a not
> Rivalled insight, be rival Italy or Greece;
> Who fired France for Mary without spot.[6]

Finishing a long letter to Canon Dixon on 13 March
1879, Hopkins adds a bare and flat postscript: "I have
been up to Godstow this afternoon. I am sorry to say
that the aspens that lined the river are everyone felled."
As in the case of the two shipwrecks, it was often a sense
of loss, touching his deep compassion, which drove Hopkins into poetry after a barren silence. Since "The Loss
of the *Eurydice*" a year before he had written only the
"May Magnificat" (and that probably at his Superior's
request). The felling of the aspens moved him into one
of the most eloquent of his lyrics, "Binsey Poplars",
warm with affection as though the trees had been his
own tender possession.

[6] On Duns Scotus's defence of the Immaculate Conception in
France, see *S.D.W.*, pp. 45, and 279.

> My aspens dear, whose airy cages quelled,
> Quelled or quenched in leaves the leaping sun,
> All felled, felled, are all felled.[7]

The blows of the axe can be heard ringing through that last line. The tall thin vertical shafts of the aspens had stood in winter like the bars of a cage striping the face of the sun.[8] How admirably the rhythm adjusts itself to the subject, changing from the sad slowness of "Not spared, not one" to the wavering

> On meadow and river and wind-wandering
> weed-winding bank.

To convince ourselves of this, let us compare for a moment much the same diction fitted to a brisker pace and more obvious rhyme-scheme:

> The aspens dear that quelled the sun,
> They have not spared them, no not one,
> Not one is left of that fresh rank
> That dandled their sandalled
> Shadow on the river and the bank.

This draft, one of many early attempts, was discarded by the poet: it was far too typical of the popular Victorian poetry which figures in contemporary magazines. Metrically, though not in its live imagery, it might have come from F. W. Faber's popular and easy-lilting "Cherwell".

We miss the true pathos of "Binsey Poplars" if we think only of a particular fringe of aspens being laid as flat as a waste, the restful inscape made featureless. Similar mutilation was in full progress all over England, ugly terrace houses or costly homes encroaching upon

---

[7] *Poems*, p. 78.

[8] Cp. Louis MacNeice, "Trapeze", which gives the metaphor of the caged lion cosmological significance, and is redolent of Hopkins.

meadows and woods. William Morris, lecturing at Birmingham within a year of the poem, denounced with grief and anger the complete disregard for beautiful trees in the planning of houses and streets: every building site was automatically cleared "as bare as the pavement", and large tracts of countryside were being ruined through sheer lack of thought. The shapely growth of fifty years could be crashed to earth in a few minutes to "improve" the prospect. Morris spoke bitterly of the destruction along the Thames at Hammersmith, where many lovely trees had been "wantonly murdered . . . amongst them some of those magnificent cedars, for which we along the river used to be famous once".[9]

The second part of "Binsey Poplars" introduces a metaphysical comparison between such injury to the great globe of the earth (as shown also in "God's Grandeur" and "Ribblesdale") and fatal damage to the microcosmic globe of the eye:

> O if we but knew what we do
>   When we delve or hew—
> Hack and rack the growing green!
>   Since Country is so tender
> To touch, her begin só slender,
> That, like this sleek and seeing ball
> But a prick will make no eye at all . . . .

The transition from the blind levelling of the landscape, by those who had no eye for nature, to loss of physical sight may have come to Hopkins through those achingly-felt passages where the poet he so much admired, John Milton, meditates on his irreparable blindness. The sight of the sun was "quenched", and instead of the "sweet approach of even or morn" there was only "a universal blank/Of Nature's works, to me expunged and rased". We hear his own lament through the lips of the blinded Samson:

[9] William Morris, *The Beauty of Life*, lecture, 19 Feb. 1880.

> Why was the sight
> To such a *tender ball* as th' eye confined,
> So obvious and so easy to be *quench'd* . . .?

No longer able to issue forth from the populous city "Among the pleasant villages and farms/Adjoining", he found himself, like Hopkins, valuing "each rural sight" more highly after he had been bereft of it.[10]

The repetitions of *rural scene* at the close of "Binsey Poplars" suggest that Hopkins was thinking of setting the poem to music. The drafts show him expanding it from a single line:

> The sweet especial rural scene . . .

to two lines and finally to the triple echoing of "scene".[11]

Two other comments from the manuscripts seem worth making. In l. 4, the word *folded* has been a little obscure, but an early reading discloses its probable intention:

> Of a fresh and following *winding* rank.

And in l.15 a discarded variant runs:

> A splinter makes no eye at all.

It would seem that another poem was already forming in his mind.

This was "The Candle Indoors".[12] Beneath the imagery of the poem lie three metaphors in the Sermon on the Mount. Christ warned his disciples to pull the *beam* out of their own eyes before worrying about the *mote* (a speck of sawdust or splinter) in another man's. In English the word *beam* suggests a play upon "eye-beam", an idea less congenial to the original New

---

[10] Milton, *P.L.*, III. 25, 48, IX. 445-51; *S.A.*, ll. 93-5.

[11] In *Poems*, Fourth Edition, p. 88, we restored a similar ending where editorial taste had previously preferred an earlier reading.

[12] *Poems*, p. 81.

Testament Greek word, δοκός (a roof-beam, a shaft or spear, but also a kind of meteor). Rays of light were sometimes thought of as arrows or spears, as in the Greek βολή or the Welsh *rhaiz,* which, said Ogilvie, meant both spear and line of light, revealing the root significance of "ray". In an interesting passage in the *Journals,* Hopkins tells how he noticed that a hot liquid *throws* off films of vapour not smoothly and continuously, but in spasms or *throes* (the two words, *throw* and *throe,* being doublets). "Candle smoke goes by just the same laws. . . . The throes can be perceived/like the thrills of a candle in the socket: this is precisely to *reech,* whence *reek*", *i.e.,* to emit smoke, throwing it off in successive films. In the next entry he observes: "What you look hard at seems to look hard at you."[13]

In "The Candle Indoors" Hopkins appears to be using the word *beam* both as a shaft of wood and a ray of light, perhaps simultaneously:

> Some candle clear burns somewhere I come by.
> I muse at how its being puts blissful back
> With yellowy moisture mild night's blear-all
>   black,
> Or to-fro tender trambeams truckle at the eye.
>
> . . . Are you beam-blind, yet to a fault
> In a neighbour deft-handed?

Beams of light were often described as consisting of "particles of light" (Ogilvie), pulsing out moment by moment. In "The Lantern out of Doors" the poet speaks of the beam from the flame as beating like drops of rain upon the "much-thick and marsh air", which suggests their exertion of pressure. In "The Candle Indoors" the commonplace "pool of light" is transformed and complicated by the interplay of imagination and feeling. The "yellowy moisture mild" (these three words form

[13] *J.P.,* 203-4.

the natural unit—the night is neither *mild* nor *tender*) which flows from the candle is, like confident love surrounded by evil, blissful, gently pushing away the "blear-all black" around it. The priest, plodding by, longs to know whether the candle is an emblem of the lives within, radiating goodness.

Line 4 is more complex. The beams striking the eye are reflected back (another metaphysical touch which would have delighted John Donne), so that they are "to-fro". The word *tram* causes much bother: no conclusive explanation can be given. *Tram* was a common mining term, used for the little low trucks which shuttled up and down the sloping galleries from the dark depths, and also for the "smooth beams of wood" on which the trams used to run. So *tram-beams* could refer both to the rays of light, going to and fro like little trucks going to and fro, and to the converging tracks or wooden truck-rails, the two slender lines which seem to join the two eyes of a man in the dark to the light-source at which he half looks as he picks his way with lowered eyelids. *Truckle* has a contributory meaning, to "run or roll"; it is a common dialect word used for things which move on little wheels or castors.[14] As Hopkins himself remarked when asked to explicate the images in "The Sea and the Skylark", "it is dreadful to explain these things in cold blood." Anyone else, commenting upon "off wild winch whirl", might have been roughly handled if he had ventured on the poet's own elaborate mechanistic account of a lark's song in terms of a flat-cored aerial reel unwinding folds of song corresponding to the musical bars![15]

[14] See William Barnes, *Tiw*, p. 245, and the *English Dialect Dictionary*. Cp. the other possible explanations offered by Fr R. V. Schoder, s.j., *Immortal Diamond*, edd. Weyand and Schoder, pp. 206-7, and Prof. W. H. Gardner, Penguin edn, etc. They suggest that *tram* means "silk thread used as a weft", and that to *truckle* is to *cower*. Neither notes that *tram* could mean "truck".

[15] *Letters*, p. 164.

In explaining to Bridges the companion poem, "The Lantern out of Doors", Hopkins had been driven to a bare mathematical exposition, but with this sonnet he declined to defend or explain the "forced" analogy.[16] The imagery returns to the candle which was its starting-point, and makes oblique allusion to another passage in the Sermon on the Mount: "Let your light so shine before men. . . ." But his own vital candle is "in close heart's vault", sending no blissful beams out into the night, and possibly, like the "fading fire", in danger of being suffocated through lack of air. In the manuscript drafts, the last line of the poem can be watched moving towards its splendid and unique compression:

And cast by conscience out for flavourless salt?

And cast by conscience out unflavoured salt?

And cast by conscience out of doors, spent salt?

And cast by conscience out, spendsavour salt?[17]

He was to return to the like ruthless self-examination in a later fragment, using the image of his heart as a dragons' lair:

There is your world within.
There rid the dragons, root out there the sin.[18]

The same dragon-imagery has given us one of the most beautiful of the Oxford sonnets, "Andromeda".[19] Andromeda, the Church, the future bride of Christ,

With not her either beauty's equal or
Her injury's, looks off by both horns of shore.

[16] See *Letters*, pp. 66-7, 85.

[17] Cp. Mt. v. 13-15, vi. 22-5, vii. 3-5. With "spendsavour" cp. Shakespeare's "lack-lustre eye", *As You Like It*, ii. vii. 21.

[18] *Poems*, p. 186.

[19] *Poems*, p. 84. The legend was a favourite one among the Victorians, *e.g.*, with Charles Kingsley and Robert Browning. See W. C. DeVane, "The Virgin and the Dragon", *Yale Review*, xxxvii (1947), pp. 33-46.

How that description of the coast focuses all thoughts upon the forsaken maiden: *horns* brings to our minds the curving shape of the bay (devoid of rescue wherever she looks), dwindling to sharp points on either side, stretched out like her own limbs. It is almost as though she has been impaled by some horned monster.[20] The word *horn* had fascinated Hopkins ever since his Oxford days, though its presence here may be due to William Morris's use of it in the identical context of Andromeda's story.[21] Perseus (invisible in his helmet) has not yet rescued his Andromeda, but one day, in the undreamt-of surprise of the Second Coming, he will alight, disarming with his "Gorgon's gear and barebill" (another *Beowulf* coinage) the fangs of the dragon and the thongs which bind her to the rock.

The curtal sonnet "Peace" bears upon its face the circumstances under which it was composed: it was drafted within two days of his leaving Oxford for the unsavoury and murky town of Bedford Leigh, to which he could scarcely be looking forward.[22] But, as another Victorian poet had discovered, "If hopes were dupes, fears may be liars"[23]; and Hopkins found, amid the coal-pits and the smoky mills, that the Lancashire Catholics were full of a "charming and cheering heartiness . . . which is so deeply comforting".[24] The comforting was mutual—a great harmony between priest and people. Moreover, he had spent long enough among North Country folk to be able to understand and to use their idioms.

Both features are illustrated in "Felix Randal".

[20] *E.g.*, the dragon: see *S.D.W.*, p. 199.

[21] William Morris, *Earthly Paradise*,—"April: The Doom of King Acrisius" (1868): "underneath the scarped cliffs of the bay/From horn to horn a belt of sand there lay."

[22] A draft is dated 2 Oct. 1879; he preached at Leigh on 5 Oct. See *Further Letters*, p. 243, and *Letters*, p. 90.

[23] A. H. Clough (1849).

[24] *Letters*, p. 97.

> Felix Randal the farrier, O is he dead then?
>   my duty all ended,
> Who have watched his mould of man, big-boned
>   and hardy-handsome
> Pining, pining, till time when reason rambled
>   in it and some
> Fatal four disorders, fleshed there, all contended?[25]

In spite of its superficial informality, almost conversational in style (toned down in transcript from "O is he gone then?"), "Felix Randal" has a richness in imagery and vocabulary which contrasts with "Peace". There is a word *mould*, for example, which was both in dialect and in poetry used for the grave—only a submerged meaning in this context. "This *mould* of man" is the Romance word, a metaphor from the casting of metal, particularly appropriate to a blacksmith's forge. Hopkins, constantly hampered throughout his own life by a body which was unequal to the demands which his urgent spirit made upon it, always admired examples of better partnerships between body and mind.

The last tercet of the sonnet is magnificently evocative of the blacksmith in his prime, care-free in his physical strength:

> How far from then forethought of, all thy
>   more boisterous years,
> When thou at the random grim forge, powerful
>   amidst peers,
> Didst fettle for the great grey drayhorse his
>   bright and battering sandal!

The sonnet holds something of the contrast in *Samson Agonistes* between the sinewed virility of the champion of Israel with his "boisterous locks" who made "useless the

<hr>

[25] *Poems*, p. 86. The first line, misprinted from the First Edn onwards, as "O he is dead then?", has been corrected in the Fourth Edn. The poem is dated "Liverpool, April 28, 1880".

forgery/Of . . . hammered cuirass", and the dishonoured state in which he is found by his friends: "See how he lies at random."[26] In this sonnet, *random* evokes the unplanned casualness of the smithy, typical of the smith's life itself. *Grim* combines reminiscences of the powerful and forbidding Satanic rebels in the smoke of Pandemonium, with its homely widespread dialect use, "dirty, grimy, covered with soot or filth". *Fettle* is surely no Shakespearian revival, but the word which every customer would use to the farrier—"make" or "mend".[27]

The last few lines are so arranged as to impart to Felix Randal the stature and splendour of the magnificent horse he is shoeing. How the rhythm beats out at times the sledge-hammer blows: *"random grim forge . . . great grey drayhorse"* (where the repeated vowels underscore the heavy strokes); we may catch, too, the quickening ring of the horseshoes on the paving. The final phase of the poem is inspired: it transforms the drayhorse from drabness to radiance as the sonnet reaches an impressive and exultant close: "his bright and battering sandal!"

The Museless slums of Liverpool produced only one more finished poem, "Spring and Fall": but a year later, while he was stationed at Glasgow, a visit to the hamlet of Inversnaid (where Arklet Water runs cascading into Loch Lomond) brought forth one of the happiest lyrics he ever wrote:

> This darksome burn, horseback brown,
> His rollrock highroad roaring down,
> In coop and in comb the fleece of his foam
> Flutes and low to the lake falls home.

How inventive the vocabulary of this brief poem is may be tested by anyone willing to search Baker's *Tennyson Concordance* for the delightful words with which "Inversnaid" abounds. Thus *darksome* is not to be found in those 1212 pages of double-column entries, for Tennyson was

[26] Milton, *S.A.*, ll. 118, 131-2, 1164.   [27] See below, p. 120.

less accustomed to giving safe harbourage in his standard
English poetry to expressive dialect words in danger of
becoming obsolete[28]; *horseback brown* lacked laureate dig-
nity, while *flitches of fern* would never have occurred to
anyone but poets (such as William Barnes and Hopkins)
who delighted in words which displayed quiddity and
personality.

The poem which in all editions since the First has
been printed after "Inversnaid" is the untitled sonnet,
"As kingfishers catch fire . . .". No fair copy of it has
been found, so that we have no certain date. It might
be as late as 1882, coinciding with his Tertianship, as
Professor Ritz suggests,[29] or as early as 1879, where I am
sometimes tempted to place it. The handwriting would
accord well enough with any date close to 1880, but the
sole surviving manuscript is a rough draft on a sheet of
cream laid paper which most closely resembles those
used for the first drafts of "The Candle Indoors" and
"Peace", both Oxford poems. Whatever its date, the
strong individual *timbre* of various Oxford bells must
have sounded sweetly in his mind when he wrote:

> As kingfishers catch fire, dragonflies draw flame;
> > As tumbled over rim in roundy wells
> > Stones ring; like each tucked string tells,
> > > each hung bell's
> Bow swung finds tongue to fling out broad its
> > name;
> Each mortal thing does one thing and the same:
> > Deals out that being indoors each one
> > > dwells;
> > Selves—goes itself; *myself* it speaks and
> > > spells,
> Crying *What I do is me*: *for that I came*.

Hopkins in his spiritual writings, perhaps following an

[28] See below, pp. 112 ff.
[29] Ritz, *Le Poète Gérard Manley Hopkins*, p. 670.

image of Duns Scotus, compares the creation to a vast
choir and orchestra, each creature sounding out its individual note towards producing the full concord which
alone could represent the perfection of God.[30] Looking,
for example, at St Winefred's Well, he rejoiced to feel
this material or sensible thing "so naturally and grace-
fully *uttering* the spiritual reason of its being"—namely,
its representation of one aspect of its Creator, the un-
failing flow of His grace, just as the lion mirrors His
strength, the sea His greatness.[31] So, too, Duns Scotus
had tried to explain how God imparts a portion of his
divine attributes to a stone.[32]

The melodious chiming in "As kingfishers catch
fire . . ." is an integral part of its meaning, and the
working draft labours consciously and persistently to
arcade these echoes. Hopkins wished to illustrate the
harmonious counter-pointing of the many individual
melodies of creation, an effect which he has simulated
through alliteration and interlocking rhymes. The first
line was fixed, but he tentatively continued:

> As tumbled over into roundy wells
> Stones ring, as every sweet string tells,
>   each bell's
> Bow answers being asked and calls its name. . . .

ring links the stones with the next example, the tensed
string, while the internal rhyme *tells*, *bells*, not only provides a run-on type of *cynghanedd sain*, but emphasises the
bond between strings and bell. The sounds, we notice,
are growing in volume, from the metallic tinkling of the

[30] *S.D.W.*, pp. 200, 351. See also Hopkins's inconclusive speculations, *S.D.W.*, pp. 122-9.

[31] *J.P.*, p. 261; cp. *S.D.W.*, p. 239.

[32] Duns Scotus; *Opus Oxoniense*, i. xxxv. 10. See C. R. S. Harris,
Duns Scotus, 2 vols., New York 1959, ii. 198, 216, etc. The Scotist
basis for this sonnet is far too complicated for discussion here. See
Fr Devlin's notes, *S.D.W.*, pp. 286, 349, and his article, "The Image
and the Word", in *The Month*, iii (1950), pp. 114-127, 191-202.

pebble clinking down the cavernous well-shaft, to the great resonating bell.

But the verbal music—alliteration, vowel-echoes, and rhyme—was not yet perfect. He changed "every sweet string tells" to "every string taxed tells", and finally hit upon the current dialect word "to tuck", so perfect a mimic of the plucked string.[33] The bells are seen before they are heard: those who have climbed Oxford towers will have observed them hanging silent and anonymous, their bows or wheels waiting to be swung, to be questioned as to their name. And then finally pencil additions at the foot of the draft give us the full onomatopoeic effect of the quickening beat of the bell as it is swayed into rhythmic motion:

> like each tucked string tells, each *hung* bell's
> Bow *swung* finds *tongue* to fling out broad its name.

How clearly-selved such a peal can be! At Stonyhurst Hopkins perceived the mellow Mitton church chimes as "orange".[34] In this draft he was so absorbed with the personality of the bell that his next line was shaped to it alone:

> Itself in every stroke it speaks and spells,
> Crying *What I do is me*: *for this I came*.

The argument of the octave, reinforced by highly poetic examples, is clear. The fiery chestnut flash of the kingfisher announces its name, though it may streak by too fast to be otherwise recognised; a jetted flame above the water reveals the darting dragonfly's course. So, too, each living thing declares its species or genus through its actions as clearly as the sound of a particular stone or string or bell in action demarks it from others of a different kind. Duns Scotus had described as *haecceitas* ("thisness"), the determinant quality which allows each

---

[33] According to the *English Dialect Dictionary*, *tuck* means touch, pull, jerk.   [34] *J.P.*, p. 218.

genus or species or individual to contribute its own note to the hierarchy of creation. Hopkins tended to call this the *self*: among brute animals he felt that the "self" or special quality lay in the species rather than in particular members of the species.[35] With man, each individual was a self "more distinctive than the taste of ale or alum, more distinctive than the smell of walnutleaf or camphor. . . . Nothing else in nature comes near this unspeakable stress of pitch."[36]

The sestet is no mere development of the octave: it announces the creation of a new species of men, separate from the rest of mankind—"Christ-men", or "just-men" (*i.e.*, "justified-men"). In the great drama of creation, their individual names are replaced by Christ's: He wears their costumes, playing the roles to which they were assigned.[37] The Father looking down on the form of this Christian or that sees beneath his outward shape the Selfhood of Christ. The poet repeats and invents words to embody this identification.

Í say more: the just man justices.[38]

Here *justices* has no simple equivalent: it is not merely "does justly", but being covered by the breast-plate or *cuirass* of Christ's justice—as he described it in a sermon about this time.[39] Some of the discarded phrases mirror his stages of thought:

Has grace and that makes all his manners graces. . . .

For Christ comes in ten thousand places,
Lives in limbs, and looks through eyes not his
With lovely yearning . . .[40]

---

[35] *S.D.W.*, p. 128.   [36] *S.D.W.*, pp. 122-3.
[37] See *S.D.W.*, p. 154.
[38] The original manuscript does not have the stress on "more" formerly printed.
[39] 26 Oct. 1879; *S.D.W.*, p. 234.   [40] Ll. 10, 12-14.

The final version is far more consistent in its angle of vision, presenting the actions or "acting" of the just as they are viewed by God.

But the "much-music" of this sonnet resonates with still other philosophical ideas and speculations—conjectures as to the very origin of the names of objects. Hopkins as an undergraduate had been somewhat attracted by the onomatopoeic theory of the birth of language,[41] to which both Farrar and Wedgwood gave support in the face of learned derision. Both quote from St Augustine's *De dialectica*, which advanced this hypothesis in its unsophisticated form. Tracing words further and further back, said St Augustine, you would come to "the point where there is a direct resemblance between the sound of the word and the thing signified".[42] This notion in turn can be traced back to the Greeks, to the analogist theory concerning the origin of nouns. Hopkins would seem to have been familiar with F. W. Farrar's *Chapters on Language* (1865), in which he outlines the concept of analogy:

Heraclitus may be regarded as the father and founder of the Analogists. He thought names were like the natural, not the artificial images of visible things, i.e., they resembled the shadows cast by solid objects, or the reflections in mirrors and on the surface of still water. "Those who use the true word do really and truly name the object, while those who do not, merely make an unintelligible noise. Hence the philosopher's object is to discover the true names which nature has assigned to things."[43]

This passage bears some verbal resemblance to a letter which Hopkins sent Bridges from Oxford in May 1879,

[41] *J.P.*, p. 5.
[42] Wedgwood, *On the Origin of Language*, 1866, p. 106.
[43] Farrar, *Chapters on Language*, p. 260.

to explain the thought behind his Purcell sonnet.[44] Here
he writes of the individualising quality within a thing
which not only stamps its species—"something distinctive, marked, specifically and individually speaking"
—but which enables it to send "abroad" its being. Thus
a face has a being "outside itself . . . by its reflection, a
body by its shadow, a man by his name, fame, or
memory". It is obvious that ideas to be found in "As
kingfishers catch fire . . ." were in his mind as early as
1879.

Although many other poems deserve as much attention and more, the limits of our present study compel a
scanter treatment. Other poems must await a further
book. We move now to those poems which followed his
Tertianship (October 1881 to September 1882), a year
of meditation and re-dedication. This he spent in the
quiet beauty of Roehampton, the luxurious trees of
Richmond Park forming, as it were, a continuation of
the charming grounds of Manresa House.[45] His first
subsequent appointment took him back to the comparative austerity of Lancashire around Stonyhurst. He had
found the country "very bare and bleak", the air
obscured by clouds "full of soot" from the huge in-
dustrial towns in the neighbourhood; "the fleeces of the
sheep are quite black with it".[46] In his sonnet "Ribblesdale" he sees the earth, which was to have become an
entire Garden of Eden for the first human beings, now
denuded of its natural coverage of wildwood by their
spendthrift heirs. The leaves may still be *throng*
("crowded") along the riverside, but elsewhere the low
grass slouches (the metaphor in *louchèd* is of a slovenly

---

[44] *Letters*, p. 83.
[45] See, *e.g.*, *Letters of the late Fr George Porter, S.J.*, 1891, pp. 9, etc.
During Hopkins's tertianship, the Rector was the Fr John Morris who
had welcomed his "Silver Jubilee" poem.
[46] *Further Letters*, pp. 234-5 (Apr. 1871), on his first arrival twelve
years earlier.

bent-back walk), an image of Nature's dissolute master, Man. The river reels like a drunkard in a land given over to "rack or wrong". The landscape, which should be glorifying God by its sheer richness, has now only a subdued beauty, and being dumb, relies upon Man (for the most part in vain) to put into words the praise which it owes the Creator. We are reminded of George Herbert's opening theme in his "Providence":

> Beasts fain would sing; birds dittie to their notes;
> Trees would be tuning on their native lute
> To thy renown: but all their hands and throats
> Are brought to Man, while they are lame and mute.

Many of Hopkins's poems, from this point onwards, provide an exposition of the blight, both upon Nature and Man himself, of which "Spring and Fall" had spoken. "On the Portrait of Two Beautiful Young People"[47] grieves at the tyrant years, "dark tramplers" of "their young delightful hour".

> What worm was here, we cry,
> To have havoc-pocked so, see, the hung-
> heavenward boughs?

> Enough: corruption was the world's first woe.
> What need I strain my heart beyond my ken?
> O but I bear my burning witness though
> Against the wild and wanton work of men.

This was one of the three themes concerning physical beauty which recur in his later verse—namely its evanescence. His classic treatment of this first theme is, of course, in "The Leaden Echo." Allied with this in both these poems is the conviction that beauty is a danger to those who wear it. The third conviction had dogged him all his life, that physical beauty was too dangerous for a devout man to contemplate intently:

[47] *Poems*, p. 196.

that theme is expounded in his sonnet "To what Serves Mortal Beauty?"

"The Leaden Echo and the Golden Echo"—meant as the maiden's chorus on fugitive beauty in his play *St. Winefred's Well*—was the only part of his tragedy which reached a high state of finish. He was wrestling with the phrasing of the dramatic portions for some seven years: lyric suited Hopkins far more naturally than did the give-and-take of dramatic interlocution. When Bridges suggested that the strange elasticity of these choral lines (varying from two syllables to over forty) could be traced to Walt Whitman, Hopkins denied all but the scantiest knowlege of his American contemporary. Instead, he quoted as his parallel and justification the choruses of Greek tragedy, in the rhythm of which he found an intellectual problem as well as inspiration.[48] In the case of Aeschylus, Hopkins believed that the choruses (though much misunderstood) in fact contained the dramatist's own interpretation of the play, his own moral to the story. Hopkins's use of the choral ode in his tragedy follows this excellent example: he makes the Welsh maidens (in what must surely have been intended as the finale of the play) apply the story of St Winefred to their own circumstances. In the dramatic fragments of *St. Winefred's Well*[49] her sweet beauty is compared to the honeysuckle. "No man has such a daughter", says her father, consumed with tremblings for the survival of the loveliness which "laces round" his heart. But after she has sacrificed her life for her honour—her head sheared from her shoulders, "lapped in her shining hair"—we find her "fleecèd bloom" of mortal beauty transformed into a never-failing spring. The fame of her beauty in body and soul will now be perpetually renewed:

[48] *Letters*, pp. 154-8; cp. p. 150, on Greek choric odes, and also p. 256, etc.
[49] *Poems*, pp. 189-93.

> As sure as what is most sure, ‖ sure as that spring
> primroses
> Shall new-dapple next year, ‖ sure as to-morrow
> morning,
> Amongst come-back-again-things, ‖ things with
> a revival, things with a recovery . . .

This is none other than the moral which Hopkins allows the Welsh maidens to draw from the miracle. "The flower of beauty, fleece of beauty" which Winefred had illustrated, can be "kept" (ambiguous word) only by freely forfeiting it.

CHAPTER IV

IN IRELAND

Early in 1884 Hopkins received from the Royal University in Dublin an invitation to accept the Chair of Classics there. But to him it seemed more like an inescapable summons: the "resolution of the senate . . . came to me, inconvenient and painful".[1] The sonnets of his Dublin days are (to me, at any rate) among the most moving in English literature. His poem, "The Blessed Virgin compared to the Air we Breathe", had ended with a prayer that she might

> Above me, round me lie
> Fronting my froward eye
> With sweet and scarless sky.[2]

But the sonnets of 1885 tell of "dark heaven's baffling ban", of eyes totally blinded to day, of a nightmare gloom in which "darksome devouring eyes" scanned his "bruisèd bones". Many have felt that Hopkins was passing in exhausted pilgrimage through the Dark Night of the Soul of which mystics and saints have left barren descriptions. But to the priest himself his experiences did not seem to correspond to any familiar ordeal on the road to sanctity: he was aware only of his own imperfections, overwrought by the image of his own utter failure, often too jaded in body, mind, and spirit to find relief in meditation or prayer. Yet out of this extremity, like drops of his own blood, came these eloquent sonnets of desolation.[3]

[1] *S.D.W.*, p. 263.   [2] *Poems*, p. 97.
[3] Cp. Fr M. C. Darcy, s.j., Foreword to John Pick, *Gerard Manley*

The blackness of the heavens is sensed nowhere more oppressively than in the sonnet beginning "I wake and feel the fell of dark, not day . . .".[4] Here is the tangible darkness which descended upon sinful Egypt at the command of Moses. *Fell* is a remarkable word, fitting its place in the line with a perfection hard to analyse. The double alliteration is obviously a help, but substituting *fall* quickly demonstrates how minor a part this plays. There are in English five homophones spelt *fell*: to my ear they interact to produce a reinforcement of pathos in this line. Professor Ritz reads it differently. Challenging the over-subtlety of Fr W. A. M. Peters in finding ambiguities within words where many of us would not suspect a double meaning, he weakens his case by referring to this line: "faut-il, parce que le poète a écrit: 'I feel the fell of dark', en donnant à ce mot le sens spensérien de *gall, bitterness*, maintenir les autres sens, plus fréquents, de *moor* ou de *pelt*? Quel avantage peut-on en retirer."[5] Althoughone can justify the interpretation of *fell* as *gall* from l. 9, yet the first image which springs to my mind is from the Psalms,[6] as the verse was expounded by St Augustine: "who stretchest out the heavens as a skin". St Augustine explained the skins which God gave to the fallen Adam and Eve as badges of their sin, because these involved the death of animals; and he connected this with the heavens, which in the darkness of our sinful world is spread out like a fell or skin, but will be rolled away in the morning of Christ's

---

Hopkins: "I am so glad that Dr Pick dismisses the superficial talk of mystic 'dark nights' when discussing the sombre sonnets of Hopkins' last years. They obviously fall into what is well known as the season of dry and dark faith, a season during which most good people are deprived of all the old sensible delights they formerly enjoyed when thinking of God".

[4] *Poems*, p. 101.

[5] Ritz, *Le Poète Gérard Manley Hopkins*, p. 629, n. 91.

[6] Ps. civ. 2. The Vulgate reads "sicut pellem", using the word from which another *fell* is derived.

H G

coming.[7] In Yorkshire and Lancashire speech *fell* was a common word for *hide* or *pelt*, though the recent English Dialect Survey shows that it has, alas, dropped out of current speech there.

The first quatrain of the sonnet tells of a journey in the horror of the night. How often must the poet have turned back to that prayer in verse, "The Pillar of the Cloud", written by one who so influenced him, John Newman:

> Lead, Kindly Light, amid the encircling gloom, . . .
> O'er moor and fen, o'er crag and torrent, till
>   The night is gone.

The long upward drag of the moorland ridge and its lurking pitfalls in the dark are surely no obscure or strained reference to find in *fell*.

Finally, the residual feeling of a "crushing blow" in *fell* is likely to spread into this line from Hopkins's contemporary sonnet "No Worst, there is None"[8]; *fell* there carries the adjectival sense of *fierce*, *cruel*:

> Fury had shrieked 'No ling—
> ering! Let me be fell: force I must be brief.'

The sonnet which we have been considering ends in a gleam of comfort, this side of perdition: an earlier reading brings back the "deathdance" of the blood in his May verses on the Blessed Virgin:

> My bones build, my flesh fills, blood feeds/this
>   curse
> Of my self stuff, by selfyeast soured. I see
> The lost are like this, and their loss/to be
> Their sweating selves, as I am mine, but worse.[9]

---

[7] Augustine, *Enarr.*, Ps. CIII, s. I, sec. 8, and Ps. v. 4. Also *Confess.*, XIII. 15, 16.   [8] Cp. "The Loss of the *Eurydice*", st. 2.

[9] The ambiguity of the last line was carefully corrected in the next version.

The demands upon his will which Hopkins increasingly made during and after his year of tertianship, and the thorniness of the path which he chose to follow, find their parallels in the deliberate preference for the uncomfortable and humanly displeasing in the lives of the saints. His commentaries on the *Spiritual Exercises of St Ignatius* throw much light upon his later sonnets in Dublin, especially when read in conjunction with the painful record of his meditations during retreats from 1884 to 1888.[10] We find him praying "to be raised to a higher degree of grace", and realising that this was "asking also to be lifted on a higher cross": the answer might not be transfiguration on a mountain top but agonising transfixion on towering "cliffs of fall". His theological insight as well as his speculations into the mysteries beyond human explanation are wonderful; but at times they err on the side of harshness. The late Fr Christopher Devlin, s.j., who seems to me to have understood the spiritual side of Hopkins with the profoundest intuition, has pointed out that the poet's beliefs are by no means always accepted Catholic doctrine. To see desire as always in opposition to duty is more the Victorianism of Arnold of Rugby than the teaching of Jesus of Nazareth.[11] Touching on a problem raised by Kierkegaard and fundamental to existentialism, Hopkins appeared to believe that God selected quite arbitrarily the physical human natures into which he put particular "selves" or "persons".[12] Even in undergraduate Oxford days before his conversion, the terror of God loomed above him more heavily than perhaps it ought, but throughout his life he strove with almost crippling spasms of will to remain faithful in the smallest particular to the highest truth he knew.

"The keener the consciousness the greater the pain"

[10] See *S.D.W.*, pp. 122-209 for his commentaries, and pp. 253-71 for his meditation notes.

[11] *S.D.W.*, pp. 116-21.   [12] *S.D.W.*, p. 146.

wrote Hopkins in a sentence which needs to be remembered as we traverse his sonnets of 1885. He envisaged the torment of souls in Hell as arising partly from their inescapable and innate desire for God, confronted with the total denial of His presence. During the Dublin years his own spiritual aspirations and prayers seemed, though only at times, to meet with a blank indifference, like the pouring-out of one's passionate heart in letters "sent/To dearest him that lives alas! away".[13] Moreover, the sense of guilt as well as guilt itself "can grow greater with increase in perfection of nature . . . there is a scale of natures, ranging from lower to higher, which height is no advantage at all to the evil self, the self which will give nature (and the higher the nature the more), a pitch to evil; so also there is a scale or range of pitch which is also infinite and terminates upwards in the directness or uprightness of the 'stem' of the godhead".[14] The terrible experience of self-loathing and hopelessness which his meditation notes reveal show how close he had come to the blinding light of Heaven, though he seemed to himself to be groping in utter darkness—a blind man for ever deprived of the day. The range of pitch in sorrow and humiliation also seemed to him to be infinite:

> No worst, there is none. Pitched past pitch of grief,
> More pangs will, schooled at forepangs, wilder wring.
> Comforter, where, where is your comforting?
> Mary, mother of us, where is your relief?[15]

The Scriptural allusions inevitably remind us of the Crucifixion of Christ, an ordeal which the saint must share. The imagery, however, strongly influenced also by Shakespeare's *King Lear*, is drawn from the great Greek tragedy in which Aeschylus tells of Prometheus's crucifixion on a precipitous crag at the very edge of the

[13] *S.D.W.*, pp. 138, 141, and *Poems*, p. 101.
[14] *S.D.W.*, pp. 147-8; my parentheses.
[15] *Poems*, p. 100.

world in punishment for his gift of fire to mankind. In the *Prometheus Desmotes* Kratos (Force) plays something of the role given to Fury in Hopkins's sonnet: he bids Hephaestus rivet without mercy the adamantine fetters on to the victim's arms and legs, smiting them with the full force of his hammer. The anvil is the age-old mountain face, against which he is immovably fastened, unable because of his immortality to escape his perpetual pain through death, unvisited by the solace of sleep. Here Hopkins finds for himself in contrast the bleak consolation in which his sonnet ends, for mortals have physical limits to their suffering.

O the mind, mind has mountains; cliffs of fall
Frightful, sheer, no-man-fathomed. Hold them cheap
May who ne'er hung there. Nor does long our small
Durance deal with that steep or deep. Here! creep,
Wretch, under a comfort serves in a whirlwind: all
Life death does end and each day dies with sleep.[16]

Hopkins was not only a seeker after spiritual perfection: he was what we would call a "perfectionist" in every circle of his life. His unpublished articles and books were stifled in their infancy by the mountainous immensity of reading and correlation which he envisaged as necessary. A more practical nature would have tackled the ascent in manageable stages, but for Hopkins the route selected was too often up the cleaves in the cliff wall. His preparation of lectures was over-thorough, so that he swamped his students in a flood of detail while his scholarly research lay stranded. He seems to have been nervously afraid of exposing himself to public criticism— an attitude which the strictures of those around and above him had moulded. As his own severest moral critic he needed to be reminded of the good advice which he had given a Liverpool congregation, that "charity begins at home: true and just selflove lies in wishing and in

[16] See Sister Mary Humiliata, *PMLA*, LXX (1955), pp. 58-68.

promoting our own best good and happiness, this is charity towards ourselves". He did from time to time remember it, as we mark in one of his most poignant sonnets:

> My own heart let me more have pity on; let
> Me live to my sad self hereafter kind,
> Charitable; not live this tormented mind
> With this tormented mind tormenting yet.[17]

The amazing hitting-power of the whole sonnet resides in the impression of artlessness, of utter sincerity, which the peculiarities of syntax and the repetitions—as though he was too exhausted to seek out petty alternatives—subconsciously confirm. This may be checked by making substitutions borrowed from other poems, for example:

> not live this tormented mind
> With this devouring mind dismembering yet.

But despite all his mental torments he could still declare: "I do not waver in my allegiance, I never have since my conversion to the Church." And this present sonnet, too, ends with a comforting reminiscence, perhaps of the occasion when he had seen "a wedge of light" breaking through between two brows of a mountain, "faintly edged, green on the right side, red on the left, as a rainbow would be, . . . skirting the brow of the hill with a glowing edge", with clouds behind it[18]—a picture of God's smile breaking through on to a sullen road and lighting "a lovely mile".

In the Fourth Edition of the *Poems* we have altered the sequence of the Dublin poems into what seems their most likely order of composition. But it must not be forgotten that some of the unfinished verses, gathered in a different section of the book, are interspersed among them. Looking through the manuscripts we find great sheets of paper with poems of contrasting mood. The

[17] *Poems*, p. 102. *S.D.W.*, p. 51. [18] *J.P.*, p. 210 (24 May 1871).

same folio which ends under the "fell of dark", begins
with a draft of his "[Ashboughs]":

> Not of all my eyes see, wandering on the world,
> Is anything a milk to the mind so, so sighs deep
> Poetry to it, as a tree whose boughs break in the sky.
>
>   . . . May
> Mells blue with snowwhite through their fringe and
>   fray
> Of greenery and old earth gropes for, grasps at
>   steep
> Heaven with it whom she childs things by.[19]

The only autograph of "No Worst, there is None",
which tells of piercing griefs and slogging anvil-blows,
has above it the first cheerful attempt at "Tom's Garland",[20] the portrait of a navvy whose iron-shod boots,
striking sparks (rockfire) from the flinty or cobbled road,
seem symbolic of his lack of sensitivity to thorny thoughts.
There are certainly advantages in being a lowly member
of the commonweal, like a "mighty foot", though it
mammocks (dialect), *i.e.*, "breaks in pieces", the mother-
ground—a hint at the destructiveness of the labourers as
well as an apt description of their pick-and-shovel work.
Only when we put these neighbouring poems together,
however, do we realise the note of envy: the lordly head
and other privileged classes may be "high hung round"
with "heaven's lights", but their homeward path each
day often edges the precipice.

Written at the same time as "Tom's Garland" and
with much the same complicated technique is "Harry
Ploughman".[21] We might treat the two portraits as
representing the town-labourer and his nobler counter-
part in the country. None of the reservations and warnings
concerning Tom Navvy are to be found in this panegyric
of rural grace and strength. Harry is the embodiment,

[19] *Poems*, p. 185.   [20] *Poems*, p. 103.   [21] *Poems*, p. 104.

not of mere muscle, but of that co-ordination of skilled timing and tireless sinews which the average book-bound reader fails to imagine necessary. The octave shows the ploughman taking up his position: his arms, grasping the wooden handles or stilts, seem a continuation of them; every muscle has its own task, like the trained members of a well-drilled crew. It is like watching a detachment smartly fall into their places, each featuring (showing by his stance) his particular job.

As the sestet opens Harry bends to take the strain, and then everything jerks abruptly into movement. The plough pitches like a ship, but the suppleness of Harry's body from the waist up enables him to keep his feet (lashed in broad bluff hide), pacing steadily behind the share and the cascading polished clods of earth. Too-studied though this piece may seem at first glance, it repays patient attention: it presents action-pictures made at close quarters by a man whose own heart was in the country.[22]

"The Shepherd's Brow",[23] however, is not about country life: it is a reaction away from the sonnets of desolation, from the cataclysmic imagery of tempests and mountains as an expression of his spiritual agony. Bridges discreetly transferred it to the section containing "Unfinished Poems and Fragments", and no doubt the three dots in l. 13 have been misinterpreted as a gap in the text by subsequent readers. But the poem is in fact complete, and these dots were introduced into the manuscript drafts to indicate a pause as the poet breaks off his heroic echoes of Shakespearian tragic actors to descend into bathos.[24] The pageantry of human life with its parade and high-sounding dignitaries is viewed on the convex bowl of a spoon, shrunk to Lilliputian size.

[22] *Further Letters*, pp. 292-3 (1 May 1888).

[23] *Poems*, p. 107.

[24] Cp. *Hamlet*, III. II. 1-32: *groundlong* suggests that *groundling* was in his mind.

If the poet had in any way exaggerated his torments in other poems, he expresses the other extreme in this derogatory sonnet.[25] The terror of God's lightning is put alongside his own puny "tempests" of grief. Ambitious Man, derisively symbolised by a bawling infant fallen on to the ground, is contrasted with the fallen angels, great even in defeat, like "giants / towers / mountains" (the manuscript hesitates between these terms). Man, who once tried to build the Tower of Babel, the top of which might reach unto heaven, is a mere empty scaffold himself, a rib-cage anxiously fed with air and water at one end, its other end hidden with Adam's shamefulness. "Human nature is so inveterate. Would that I had seen the last of it", he had written from Lancashire.[26] "Our whole civilization is dirty, yea filthy", he exclaimed in 1889, ending with references to the "traitors" whose names were blazoned as leaders of England and Ireland:

Man Jack the man is, just; his mate a hussy.[27]

Stimulating though this poem is, with a tang rare in Hopkins, a vital factor is missing. Man is more than "Jack, joke, poor potsherd, patch, matchwood", as he had indeed eloquently acknowledged in a truly magnificent poem which, though composed a little earlier, we have reserved for the close of this chapter: "That Nature is a Heraclitean Fire and of the Comfort of the Resurrection".[28] In this sonnet, too, man is seen from a distance, no larger than a spark, and as shortlived. The great cosmic process of reversible change is shown as applying to everything else in Nature except to "her bonniest, dearest to her, he clearest-selvèd spark Man". Hopkins uses the ideas of one of the most poetic among the Greek philosophers, Heraclitus of Ephesus: but where Hera-

[25] Bridges destroyed two letters from Hopkins contemporary with this sonnet: *Letters*, p. 303, n. 3.
[26] *Letters*, p. 110 (26 Oct. 1880).
[27] *Letters*, pp. 299-300.   [28] *Poems*, p. 105.

clitus had been as cryptic as the Delphic Oracle, Hopkins expands into loving detail the delightful counter-
poised strife of fire and water. The Greek philosopher
had seen as the basic constituent of the world an element
which he called "fire", displayed in its purest form in
lightning, but also filling the shining æther which surrounded the earth. It was to be found in the souls of men,
though too often diluted by water, for although virtuous
souls might become part of the great cosmic fire, the
weak soul might be drowned by becoming all water
instead of a part of the divine substance.

This cosmic fire had a passion to change its form: it
fed upon the moist exhalations from the earth, drawing
clouds into the air by its heat, at the same time itself becoming water and falling into the sea and on to the dry
land. In this way nature presented a perpetual balanced
cycle, the measures of the three forms of matter being
kept in equilibrium. Heraclitus, however, was credited
by the later Stoics with the belief that a great worldfire
devoured everything from time to time, a notion which
Hopkins incorporates here as being in line with Christian
thinking.[29]

The poem is masterly in its artistic three-fold division.
The first nine lines depict the action of the fire in
evaporating the water from the ground after a storm.
The clouds fly up from the earth, as though they were
"puffballs" and "tufts" which she had grown, and
"then" (mark the stages) race each other across the sky.
They are somewhat tipsy with moisture—"heaven-
roysterers, in gay-gangs they throng"—a phrase which
is remarkably Anglo-Saxon in its shape. The "bright
wind" seems a curious term until we remember that
Heraclitus identified his fire with the *aither*, the bright
or upper air (from *aithein*, "to shine"). This "bright
wind" is the agent of the Heraclitean fire, drying out the

[29] See G. S. Kirk and J. E. Raven, *The Presocratic Philosophers*,
Cambridge 1957, pp. 182-215.

liquid mud in successive stages, making it earth again.

Million-fuelèd,¹ nature's bonfire burns on.

The atmosphere abruptly saddens as we are swept back into a night of storm, in which the starry lights of men are doused as though they were no more than sparks from two rocks dinted together. A liquid darkness, like primeval chaos itself, swallows up their existence:

> O pity and indig¹nation! Manshape, that shone
> Sheer off, disseveral, a star,¹ death blots black
> out; nor mark
> Is any of him at all so stark
> But vastness blurs and time¹ beats level.

This process seems irreversible. But the drowning heart is cheered, not by rescue, but by the realisation that the fires and waters of change can act only upon the transient parts of man: within him he has the "diamond" spirit, the adamant, the unconquerable, which will remain when "world's wildfire" or "the residuary worm"[30] have consumed the rest. As Heraclitus enigmatically declared: "immortals are mortals, mortals are immortals". The immortal Christ put on our mortality in order that we might put on His immortality. To the Christian the Heraclitean fires of renewal bring no lasting joy or peace: his great hope must lie in the "Comfort of the Resurrection".

[30] Cp. Shakespeare, Sonnet CXLVI ("Shall worms, inheritors of this excess,/Eat up thy charge . . . ?")

CHAPTER V

SPRUNG RHYTHM

"Reading over what I have written above," confessed Hopkins, after attempting to explain the principles of Sprung Rhythm in a letter to Canon Dixon, "I find it very hurried and confused: I hope you may gather some meaning out of it. I shd. add that the word Sprung which I use for this rhythm means something like *abrupt* and applies by rights only where one stress follows another running, without syllable between."[1] Although Sprung Rhythm derived its name from the juxtaposed stresses which form its most prominent feature, it cannot be identified solely by means of them, for accents may be brought together by the simple process of reversing feet, or "counterpointing" as Hopkins called it; for example, in a Miltonic line which he loved to quote:

Home to his mother's *house private* return'd.[2]

His own poems in "standard" or "running rhythm" were studded with like examples, usually produced by substituting an accentual trochee ($' ^\times$) for an iamb ($^\times '$):

Lovely the *woods, waters*, meadows, combes, vales. . . .[3]

---

[1] *Correspondence*, p. 23 (27 Feb. 1879); "Author's Preface", *Poems*, p. 46.

[2] *J.P.*, p. 282; *Letters*, p. 38; *Correspondence*, p. 15. In the following examples, adjacent accents are printed in italics. Hopkins did not consistently distinguish between "accent" and "stress".

[3] *Poems*, p. 68.

The singularly refreshing effect of a sonnet by Hopkins is frequently due to the skill and boldness of his counter-point.

A "sprung rhythm" may be with more justice said to occur when an accented monosyllable occupies the time of a full foot: the reader then has the sensation of having to *spring* from one stress to another over an intervening gap. Hopkins had found scores of examples in earlier verse, and had pointed some out to his students at Manresa House when he was Professor of Rhetoric.[4] His instances were mostly taken from dipodic measures, the nature of which Coventry Patmore had analysed in a paper which Hopkins was slow to discover: "English Metrical Critics".[5] Thus in a trochaic tetrameter of the pattern

> Tongues I'll hang on every tree

we find in Shakespeare:

> Why should *this* ∧ *de*sert be?[6]

a line mistakenly "restored" by editors who could not believe that the monosyllabic foot ("*this*∧") was intentional. Hopkins, convinced that it was, had begun experimenting with such abrupt rhythms himself as early as his undergraduate days:

> His cap shall *be* ∧ *shi*ning fur . . .[7]

[4] *J.P.*, pp. 277-8; cp. *Letters*, p. 156.

[5] *North British Review*, Aug. 1857; reprinted with changes as "Essay on English Metrical Law", prefacing Coventry Patmore's *Amelia*, 1878; then as Appendix to his *Poetical Works*, 1886, II. 216-67. For Hopkins's comments, see, *e.g.*, *Letters*, pp. 119-20 (1881), 204, 269.

[6] *As You Like It*, III. II. 133; quoted, *J.P.*, p. 278; *Letters*, p. 24; *Correspondence*, p. 14.

[7] "Daphne", 1 Sep. 1865, *Poems*, p. 166.

and (a little later):

Quínces, loók, ʌ whén not óne. . . .[8]

Now such sprung rhythms do not constitute Sprung Rhythm. The essence of Sprung Rhythm is the accept-ance of unlimited substitution, whereby in a line of a given number of feet, that number of primary accents is permitted, accompanied by as few or as many un-accented or slack syllables as the poet pleases. How these feet are divided does not matter, whether they are "rising" (the stress coming last), "falling" (the reverse), or "rocking" (the stress lying in the middle); but by 1884, when he wrote his famous "Author's Preface" to the album of his poems collected by Bridges into Ms. B, he had come to prefer the equivalent of musical bars in which "the accent or the chief accent always comes first".[9] This statement surely implies that a foot may contain two stresses, provided that one is a little weaker than the other—a modification commonly overlooked. Ordinary running rhythm allows such almost equal stresses itself. Many of Hopkins's sprung lines require the recognition of weak stresses for satisfactory analysis.

This explanation of Sprung Rhythm, however, sug-gests that a poem could legitimately be made up of a prose passage cut into line-lengths, each measured only by its number of heavy stresses. Bridges at first concluded that there was "no conceivable licence" which Hopkins would not be prepared to justify under his new system.[10] Students of Hopkins have often remarked upon the apparent anomaly that the priest who tended to apply to himself the strictest limitations of the law, should as a poet have broken so many conventions. But Hopkins contrasted the free verse and free morality of a Walt Whit-

---

[8] "Lines for a Picture", (?) 1868, *Poems*, p. 36.
[9] See *Poems*, p. 45: cp., however, *Letters*, pp. 155-6; *Correspondence*, pp. 39-40.   [10] *Letters*, p. 44.

man with the obedience to God's laws in rhythm and in nature for which he himself was always striving.[11] Writing about the "Rondeliers" who were experimenting with exotic forms of verse, he drops a remark which appears on the surface purely facetious: "It seems that triolets and rondels and rondeaus and chants royal and what not *and anything but serving God* are all the fashion."[12] We find him glossing this a few days later when he tells Bridges that "all English verse, except Milton's, almost, offends me as 'licentious'." The word has strong moral overtones. "With all my licences, or rather laws, I am stricter than you and I might say than anybody I know."[13] Just as he had sought in his scrutiny of nature to identify natural *laws* of being visibly expressed, so he sought for the most "natural" rhythms. Milton's verse, he tells Dixon, "seems something necessary and eternal (so to me does Purcell's music)".[14] Milton was an Aristotle in the realm of poetic technique. Like a theologian formulating a new doctrine out of ideas found scattered among the Church Fathers, Hopkins set out to develop to their logical limits the prosodic systems latent in Shakespeare and Milton and hinted-at in the choruses of Greek plays as he analysed their metres. Sprung Rhythm, indeed, appeared to him "a better and more natural principle than the ordinary system"; "nature ... seems to prompt it of itself" mainly because it approached the rhythms of everyday speech.[15]

The importance which Hopkins attached to form and structure I have discussed elsewhere.[16] If in theory he

---

[11] See *Letters*, pp. 154-8.

[12] *Letters*, p. 43 (my italics); cp. pp. 49-50.

[13] *Letters*, pp. 44-5 (21 Aug. 1877).

[14] *Correspondence*, p. 13 (5 Oct. 1878); cp. *Letters*, pp. 234-5.

[15] *Correspondence*, pp. 14, 21; *Letters*, p. 46. For discussions of the origin of Sprung Rhythm, see W. H. Gardner, *Gerard Manley Hopkins*, II. 98 ff., and Fr W. Ong, s.j., "Sprung Rhythm and the Life of English Poetry", pp. 105 ff.

[16] See N. H. MacKenzie, "Hopkins among the Victorians".

ignored the junctures at the ends of lines,[17] scanning
continuously from the beginning of a stanza to its end,
in practice he almost invariably inserted the "necessary
rhymes" so that the sense of structure might not be
lost.[18] But the natural laws which he was seeking to
follow disclosed themselves only to the most sensitive ear:
they were no Levitical Code comprising innumerable
regulations. He thought instead of "period-building",
in which the strengths of the feet, however varied in their
constituent syllables, should be cunningly balanced
against each other. Moreover, time entered into the
complex, though he does not seem to have accepted any
rigid isochronous theory of the spacing-out of stresses.
"Since the syllables in sprung rhythm are not counted,
time or equality in strength is of more importance than
in common counted rhythm, and", he added, referring
to Bridges's experiments in a similar rhythm, "your times
or strengths do not seem to me equal enough."[19] In so
subjective a matter, with each man's ear acting as his
poetic dynamometer, such criticism is impossible to
refute.

Three months earlier, not altogether consistently, he
had told Dixon that whereas classical hexameters
allowed substitution on the principle of equal lengths or
times, Sprung Rhythm was "founded upon an easily felt
principle of *equal strengths*". He invented a delightfully
improbable tragic line in which four successive pairs of
feet offered mutual counterparts in their separate
rhythmic weights: "sanguinary consequences . . ." (obviously ignoring bipodic scansion, which would make these
double feet), "terrible butchery, frightful slaughter, fell
swoop." The line opens with two first pæons and ends
with two monosyllabic feet.[20] "The total strength of

[17] "Author's Preface", *Poems*, p. 48; *Correspondence*, p. 40.
[18] Note on "The Wreck of the *Deutschland*", Ms. A, printed in
Poems, p. 256; cp. *Letters*, p. 246.
[19] *Letters*, pp. 81-2 (26 May 1879).   [20] *Correspondence*, p. 22.

sanguinary is no more than that of *terrible* or of *frightful* or of *fell* and so on of the substantives too." He held that a monosyllabic foot gathers into its isolated stress the strength which in a longer foot is distributed between the stress and the slack syllables belonging to it. Great skill and musical judgment lie behind a stanza in Hopkins: his ear very seldom betrayed him into a dull passage.

Hopkins's experimental theories and practice were inevitably liable to contain inconsistencies and to be modified as he developed. If he had found the leisure to prepare for publication the full treatise which he planned on English versification in general and Sprung Rhythm in particular, he would have been led to think out his principles more exactly. As it was, his explanations are casually scattered over the years, among hundreds of pages of correspondence of which he could keep no copy. Returning to one of his poems after an interval, he tended to read its melodies a little differently: the extra-metrical phrases of which he made a minor feature, (calling them "hangers" or "outrides") are often changed in a later manuscript.[21] Thus in "Felix Randal", in which Professor Gardner used to claim that "there are altogether 15 outrides, many of which are necessary guides to the rhythm",[22] Mss. A and B between them show 18 different outrides, upon only 10 of which they can agree. And with a rhythm in which a foot can absorb into its total strength three or four or even six slack syllables, only the subjective and variable judgment of poet and reader can guess whether a foot will be over-weighted or not by including within its feet the group of hurried syllables excluded from them as an outride in some autograph. The presence of outrides in the "falling pæonic" rhythm of "The Caged Skylark" has always puzzled me, nor can I always detect the "slight pause" which should follow an outride.[23] But these scarcely

---

[21] *Letters*, p. 45; *Correspondence*, p. 15.
[22] *Poems*, Third Edn, p. 237.   [23] *Poems*, p. 293.

affect the demonstrable success of his Sprung Rhythm
and his poising of phrase against phrase.

This flexible theory of balanced strengths and "period-
building" seems to me to owe an unrecognised debt to a
remarkable essay in prosody whose appearance may, in
fact, have decided Hopkins that it was not worth his
while working up for publication his new theory of
Sprung Rhythm. In December 1874 (a year before "The
Wreck of the *Deutschland*"), John Addington Symonds
brought out a paper on "The Blank Verse of Milton"
in *The Fortnightly Review*.[24] Symonds had been a Balliol
man; Hopkins knew his sister, who had married the
Balliol tutor, T. H. Green.[25] He also knew the theories
which Symonds had advanced. Writing to Bridges on
Sprung Rhythm, Hopkins observed:

> The choruses of Samson Agonistes are still more re-
> markable: I think I have mastered them and may
> some day write on the subject. However J. A. Symonds
> has written a paper on Milton's verse somewhere and
> it has, I see, received attention of late.[26]

Symonds analysed Milton in terms of "periods" rather
than feet, of balanced weights of emphasis rather than
metrical equivalents:

> A verse may often have more than ten syllables, and
> more or less than five accents; but it must carry so
> much sound as shall be a satisfactory equivalent for
> ten syllables, and must have its accents so arranged as
> to content an ear prepared for five.[27]

He spoke about the need to preserve "the balance and
proportion of syllables", while varying "their relative

[24] Reprinted with two other essays on blank verse in the Appen-
dices to his *Sketches and Studies in Italy*, 1879—the text quoted here.
[25] *Further Letters*, p. 152.   [26] *Letters*, p. 38 (3 Apr. 1877).
[27] J. A. Symonds, "The Blank Verse of Milton", in *Sketches and
Studies in Italy*, p. 416.

weight and volume, so that each line in a period shall carry its proper burden of sound, but the burden shall be differently distributed in the successive verses".[28] Symonds repeatedly alludes to *periods*[29]; it is interesting to note that Hopkins on one occasion referred to his Sprung Rhythm as "my period-building (or whatever we are to call it)".[30] Symonds rejected the dull mechanical analyses of the nineteenth-century handbooks—how dull only those of us can witness who have toiled through the extant works on prosody from Dr Johnson onwards.[31] Symonds seemed to orthodox prosodists to reject the very foundations of versification,[32] but his recipe for achieving harmonious verse was parallel to Hopkins's own:

by forcing the accentuation of prominent mono-syllables and gliding over successive liquid sounds, by packing one line with emphatic words so as to retard its movement, by winging another with light and hurried polysyllables, and by so adapting words to sense, and sense to rhythm, that pauses, prolongations, and accelerations, absolutely necessary for the under-standing of the matter, evoke a cadence of apparently unstudied melody. In this prosody the bars of the musical composer, where different values from the breve to the demi-semiquaver find their place, suggest perhaps a truer basis of measurement than the longs and shorts of classic quantity.[33]

Here we have a striking analogy with the feet of Sprung Rhythm, where the monosyllabic foot corresponds with the breve or semi-breve, and the hurried seven-syllabled

[28] Symonds, *op. cit.*, p. 417.
[29] *E.g.*, *op. cit.*, pp. 403, 414, 419.
[30] *Letters*, p. 82.
[31] Steele's *Prosodia rationalis*, 2nd edn (1779), and Roe's *Principles of Rhythm* (1823) are welcome exceptions.
[32] See, *e.g.*, T. S. Osmond, *English Metrists*, 1907, pp. 168-9.
[33] Symonds, "The Blank Verse of Milton", in *Sketches and Studies in Italy*, p. 417.

foot which Hopkins thought he had included in "The Wreck of the *Deutschland*" corresponds to a bar with crotchets or quavers.[34] As we read Symonds the magic of "The Windhover" seems even more apposite an exemplification than the choruses in Milton.

In an explanatory note to the Reader,[35] prefacing "The Wreck of the *Deutschland*", Hopkins discusses the infinite variability of the stresses in his poem:

> Be pleased, reader, since the rhythm in which the following poem is written is new, strongly to mark the beats of the measure. . . . Only let this be observed in the reading, that, where more than one syllable goes to a beat, then if the beating syllable is of its nature strong, the stress laid on it must be stronger the greater the number of syllables belonging to it, the voice treading and dwelling.[36]

We may note that this seems to contradict his account of the allocation of strengths in his letter to Dixon of 27 February 1879.[37] It is, however, a refinement on the generalisation there. He goes on to say that if the stressed syllable is

> by nature light, then the greater the number of syllables belonging to it the less is the stress to be laid on it, the voice passing flyingly over all the syllables of the foot and in some manner distributing among them all the stress of the one beat.[38]

The complications into which these subtleties lead us we have no space to explore.[39] In this scanty survey of an immense subject we may, however, remark that unless we introduce medium stresses quite freely (a practice for

---

[34] *Letters*, p. 45.
[35] Published in full for the first time in *Poems*, pp. 255-6.
[36] *Poems*, pp. 255-6.　　　　　　　　[37] *Correspondence*, pp. 21-2.
[38] *Poems*, p. 256.　　　　　　　　[39] See also *Correspondence*, p. 41.

which we have some warrant in the "Author's Preface"),
many of the lines in "The Wreck of the *Deutschland*" and
elsewhere will seem to contain a larger number of important syllables than the stresses allowed by the poet's
stanzaic pattern. Take "The Wreck of the *Deutschland*",
st. 6:

> Not out of his bliss
> Springs the stress felt.

The first line is allotted two stresses, the second three.
This limitation seemed fairer in the first manuscript
version:

> And not from his bliss
> Springs the stress that is felt.

The poet recognised only three main stresses in each of
these lines:

> Breathe, arch and original Breath . . . .
>
> Breathe, body of lovely death . . . .
>
> Our King back, Oh, upon English souls! . . .
>
> Of the Yore-flood, of the year's fall . . . .
>
> Thou hadst glory of this nun? . . .[40]

At times the stresses seem to be awarded through the
arbitrary elimination of some claimants, as when he
distributed only four accents among:

> Pride, rose, prince, hero of us, high-priest.[41]

The alliteration provides no reliable clue: *high* is stressed,
but not *hero*. Are there not several lines in "The Windhover" which demand six accents rather than five?

It is surely no service to Hopkins to claim for the useful
techniques of analysis presented in his Sprung Rhythm

---

[40] "The Wreck of the *Deutschland*", sts. 25, 35, 32, 30.
[41] *Op. cit.*, st. 35.

H H*

theory an unassailable perfection which no other prosodic system before or since his day can be said to have
achieved. It may well be that his poetry (however pleasing to our ears) is not as free as he had thought from the
charge of being "licentious". What is important is the
fundamental soundness of his two main drives—well in
line with modern thinking— to bring poetry closer to the
living language of men, and to achieve perpetual originality without loss of form. George R. Stewart, a great
twentieth-century prosodist, can hardly be accused of
having derived his notions from Hopkins, since he does
not quote him even in his chapter on "The Monosyllabic Foot". Yet the final paragraph of his *Modern
Metrical Technique* (1922) analyses the main trend of prosodic evolution as the replacement of an easy metrical
convention by a difficult technique, one designed "to
harmonize constant metrical variety with underlying
metrical regularity. One motivating factor has been the
desire to combine metrical structure with natural speech
rhythm." This latter objective is seen by T. S. Eliot as a
characteristic of some of the most important poetic
revolutions in all ages, including the work of Hopkins.
"The music of poetry . . . must be a music latent in the
common speech of its time."[42] Hopkins seems in theory
to be following Wordsworth when he defends Sprung
Rhythm primarily because "it is the nearest to the
rhythm of prose, that is the native and natural rhythm
of speech".[43] But in practice he wished for a rhetorical
delivery of his poems. Unlike ordinary conversation, the
memorable utterances of poetry arise because words have
been selected for their sound as well as their sense, and
been built moreover into significant shapes. We may end
where Hopkins's theorising about poetry may be said to
begin, with the definition which he gave his students at
Manresa House in 1873-4:

[42] T. S. Eliot, *On Poetry and Poets*, London 1957, pp. 31-3.
[43] *Letters*, p. 46.

Poetry is speech framed for contemplation of the mind
by the way of hearing or speech framed to be heard for
its own sake and interest even over and above its
interest of meaning. Some matter and meaning is
essential to it but only as an element necessary to support and employ the shape which is contemplated for
its own sake.[44]

The interaction between form and statement is too intimate to yield to any physical analysis. As Winifred
Nowottny has recently observed:

The verse system itself contains highly-differentiated
"events", such as the bold inversion of a foot, the delicate balance of a line, because it is in itself a system of
many components giving rise to many expectations,
many emphases, many crises and resolutions of pattern. . . . The fineness with which we appreciate these
values and relate them to one another is, like most
other advanced operations of the human mind, beyond our powers of recapitulation in verbal terms.[45]

When these inter-relationships are as profoundly
achieved as they are in the major poetry of Hopkins,
we may expect our metrical pressure-gauges and
chronometers to yield us only a very partial insight into
his success.

[44] "Poetry and Verse", *J.P.*, p. 289.
[45] W. Nowottny, *The Language Poets Use*, London 1962, pp. 115-6.

CHAPTER VI

ENRICHMENT FROM DIALECT

Hopkins's undergraduate days fell in a phase of philological study when the varieties of English provincial
speech were receiving enthusiastic if overdue attention.[1]
In the preface to a work published in the year in which
Hopkins entered Balliol, William Barnes wrote:

> In searching the word stores of the provincial speech-
> forms of English we cannot but behold what a wealth
> of stems we have overlooked at home, while we have
> drawn needful supplies of words from other tongues;
> and how deficient is even English itself without the
> synonyms which our land-folk are ready to give it.[2]

In the "Foresay" to a later book, Barnes spoke of the
"mighty wealth of English words" which the English
Dialect Society had begun to bring forth,

> words of meanings which dictionaries of book-English
> should, but cannot give, and words which should be
> taken in hundreds (by careful choice) into our Queen's
> English. If a man would walk with me through our
> village, I could show him many things of which we
> want to speak every day, and for which we have words
> of which Johnson knew nothing.[3]

[1] The American author George Marsh's *Lectures on the English
Language*, 1858, with which Hopkins was familiar, was an exception.
Marsh was afraid that American English would weaken itself into
dialects: see *J.P.*, pp. 284, 287 and n.

[2] W. Barnes, *Grammar and Glossary of the Dorset Dialect* (1863),
p. 9.

[3] W. Barnes, *An Outline of English Speech-Craft* (1878).

As his own contribution towards the preservation of valuable dialect words, Barnes published three volumes of Dorset poems (1844, 1859, and 1862)—poems which Hopkins read and admired while he was still at Oxford.[4] The stimulus and direction which he received from this early influence have probably been considerably underestimated.

During the course of his boyhood and his career as a Jesuit, Hopkins enjoyed many changes of scene which brought him into contact with the living English of the farm-worker and rural tradesman. His family spent long holidays in the Isle of Wight and other parts of Hampshire; his grandmother came from Manley, near Tiverton, and spoke with a recognisable Devonshire accent.[5] As a novice he did manual work in the fields and orchards around Manresa, under the supervision of lay brothers full of country lore and phraseology.[6] Much of his training and parish work lay in Lancashire: moreover, as he remarked, many of his fellow Jesuits were north-countrymen.[7] Through the last five years of his life he was in Ireland, and during his visits to different Jesuit houses in Ireland he collected words for the great *English Dialect Dictionary* then being compiled. His "unpublished manuscript collection" is acknowledged in the bibliography of that work, but Wright does not seem to have found Hopkins's contribution of distinct value, and Irishisms which Hopkins had gathered from Br Yates,[8] such as "*soak it* almost = lump it," and "*crackawly* = simpleton", do not figure in Wright's published work.[9]

But all through his life Hopkins retained his curiosity about dialect words and went out of his way to gather

---

[4] *Letters*, p. 87. [5] *Further Letters*, p. 89.
[6] See, *e.g.*, *J.P.*, pp. 190-1.
[7] *Further Letters*, p. 240. [8] *J.P.*, p. 198.
[9] *Further Letters*, p. 184, contains ref. to Hopkins's correspondence with Prof. Joseph Wright, the editor of the *E.D.D.* See W. W. Skeat's abrupt letter to Hopkins, *Further Letters*, pp. 431-2.

them. From one lay brother he learned terms used in ploughing[10]; from another farmhand he records the intricate vocabulary which differentiated each successive stage in cutting and gathering the hay, from the *swathe* and *strow* to the *rickles* and *placks*, ready for carting or carrying.[11] When Bridges challenged his use of *bole* in a poem as an obsolete word (as dictionaries then classified it), Hopkins defended it as a technical word in current use among timber merchants.[12]

Early in his *Journals*[13] we find him making intelligent comparison between his Elizabethan reading and current rural speech. "In Isle of Wight dialect to *gally* is to harry, annoy, and Shakspere has *gallow* in same sense." The reference is to the earliest known written appearance of the word, in *King Lear*:

> the wrathful skies
> Gallow the very wanderers of the dark,
> And make them keep their caves. . . . Man's
>   nature cannot carry
> Th' affliction nor the fear.[14]

Hopkins was correct in presuming that the two words were variants of each other, but he had apparently not heard *gally* in a sufficient number of contexts to realise that its basic meaning is "to terrify" rather than "to annoy".[15] Nor did he correct his first impressions. Some seventeen years later he described the difficulties of composing when faced with parish work in Liverpool: "I never could write; time and spirits were wanting; one is so fagged, so harried and gallied up and down."[16] Here

[10] *J.P.*, p. 237.

[11] *J.P.*, pp. 212-3; cp. p. 191.

[12] *Letters*, p. 52.

[13] *J.P.*, p. 16 (1864).

[14] *King Lear*: III. II. 44.

[15] See *E.D.D.*: cp. also such special authorities as W. Barnes, *Tiw* (1862), p. 78 ("*Gally*—west country, to frighten"), or Sarah Hewlett, *The Peasant Speech of Devon* (1892), p. 80 ("Gally—to scare: 'They've gallied tha old feller tü death purty near!'").

[16] *Letters*, p. 110 (26 Oct. 1880).

the parallel words indicate to us the meaning it held for Hopkins more accurately than reference to a dictionary would.

Much of the curious "poetic" language in Hopkins's *Journals*, which most readers only half comprehend, is in fact drawn from dialect. Whereas in his poetry he planted a strange word among near-synonyms from which it could draw clarity and to which it could lend its own virile force, no such need governed the phrasing of his private *Journals*. Scores of examples might be cited. An obvious one occurs in his description of a handful of bluebells: "if you draw your fingers through them they are lodged and struggle/with a shock of wet heads".[17] Here the Shakespearian sense of *lodged*—applied to corn or grass beaten down by rain or wind—a significance which had been retained in ordinary farming parlance —is extended from its common use. His "*shock* of wet heads" is influenced by the Devonshire word for a stook of corn.[18]

At other times his more literary or phonetic spelling of dialect words successfully cloaks their origin. Holidaying in Switzerland, he remarked that the beginning of the Rhone glacier—"a smoothly-moulded bed in a pan or theatre of thorny peaks"—was like "bright-*plucked* water swaying in a pail".[19] This may well be a normalised spelling of the Scottish and north-country *plookit*, "pimply", from *plook*, or *pluke*—a pimple or spot on the skin.

The journals are full of imaginative descriptions, all the more effective because of their individual vocabulary. At Stonyhurst one summer day Hopkins wrote:

Bright, with a high wind blowing the crests of the trees before the sun and fetching in the blaze and dousing it again. In particular there was one light raft of beech which the wind footed and strained on, ruffling the

[17] *J.P.*, p. 209.   [18] *J.P.*, p. 251.   [19] *J.P.*, p. 178.

leaves which came out in their triplets threaded round with a bright brim like an edge of white ice, the sun sitting at one end of the branch in a pash of soap-sud-coloured gummy bim-beams rowing over the leaves but sometimes flaring out so as to let a blue crust or platter from quite the quick of the orb sail in the eye.[20]

"A *pash* of soap-sud-coloured *bim-beams*" is a delightful phrase, even when we cannot be exactly sure of its origins. *Pash* is a dialect word for a medley or collection of crushed or broken fragments, a pulpy mass, a sudden rush of water, a puddle. Hopkins uses it not very precisely, *e.g.* in "tufts and pashes of grass".[21] But *bim-beams* is more elusive, seeming to be a rationalising of the Somerset *bimboms*, originally referring to church bells, but applied to anything dangling down, such as tassels, drops of rain hanging from a rail, or icicles.[22]

Tretted is another Hopkinsian touch. We read of "tretted mossy clouds",[23] of waterfalls "gaily sprigged, tretted and curled edges dancing down, like the crispiest endive", where the editors have every excuse for having misread the manuscript as "fretted".[24] Chambers in his *Book of Days* (1863) had reminded Victorians of the old *trete bread* made of coarse wheat meal from which only the roughest bran had been removed. *Treat* or *trete* was a current dialect word for the second quality of bran. That this is the origin of *tretted* is confirmed a few pages later when we come upon another waterfall: "In the second fall when facing the great limbs in which the water is packed saw well how they are tretted like open sponge or light bread-crumb where the yeast has supped in the texture in big and little holes."[25]

The influence of dialect upon Hopkins's prose vocabulary cannot be fully handled here, but before we go on

[20] *J.P.*, p. 233 (18 Jul. 1873).
[22] *E.D.D.*
[24] *J.P.*, p. 173.

[21] *J.P.*, p. 243.
[23] *J.P.*, pp. 142, 156.
[25] *J.P.*, p. 177.

to like elements in his poems we should observe again that the compiling of glossaries is beset with snares. A dialect is subject to the disrupting effects of other forms of English. The field-workers in Professor Orton's *Survey of English Dialects*[26] took elaborate precautions to select old men of sixty or over for their informants, and to check every word and its connotation from others in that and neighbouring areas. When Professor Joseph Wright set out to edit the *English Dialect Dictionary*, for which an enormous pile of material had already been collected, he rapidly concluded that for safe scholarship he needed at least twice as many examples. He had over a million and a half slips, each giving a word in context, before he began publication, and even then he had to write thousands of letters to selected correspondents to satisfy himself of the authenticity of the meaning suggested. He rejected many words for lack of evidence.[27] It is interesting to note that the new *Survey of English Dialects* is uncovering terms which even the monumental *English Dialect Dictionary* did not record.[28]

Hopkins had no such elaborate and scholarly teams to reinforce his solitary efforts. His informants were sometimes wrong. He notes down:

> Trees sold 'top and lop': Br. Rickaby told me and suggests *top* is the higher, outer, and lighter wood good for firing only, *lop* the stem and bigger boughs when the rest has been lopped off, used for timber.[29]

In fact, *lop* refers to what has been lopped off and not what is left: "Top or lopwood" is a more revealing phrase.

[26] Leeds 1962-.
[27] See the beginning of each volume, and the Supplement, for words held back.
[28] See *e.g.*, Vol. I, Pt I, under *rung*. On the other hand, many words given by Wright seem to have died out in the meanwhile.
[29] *J.P.*, p. 191.

Hopkins is almost certainly wrong when he records *duffer* as meaning "an ass (literally)" in Cumberland.[30] But he may have picked up a stray variant when he reports (scrupulously quoting his source) "Mr Cleave says they call a wooden bridge over the river a *clamp*".[31] His informant was a Devon carpenter living in Bovey Tracey, but I have found no confirmation anywhere of this equivalent of the West Country *clam* or *clammer*.[32]

Although Hopkins's poetry contains dozens of words which he found in common village use, their identity has been obscured by their earlier appearance in Elizabethan English. Even as good a scholar as Professor W. H. Gardner has classified most of them as effective archaisms.[33] Hopkins had condemned those who tamely adopted Shakespeare's vocabulary, reproducing "diction which in him was modern and in them is obsolete"—"it destroys earnest: we do not speak that way".[34] A little archaism (he conceded) provided flavour—and he was prepared to sprinkle Spenserian or earlier words here and there in his own work. But most of the examples which have been quoted by critics as Shakespearian or Spenserian were in fact used by the common people in Victorian England. Very occasionally these turn out to be terms of recent origin—*chevy* entered our vocabulary in the nineteenth century, and in the sense used by Hop-

[30] *J.P.*, p. 15. Such a literal application is not included in *E.D.D.* nor known to Prof. Orton, Dr Halliday, and their team.

[31] *J.P.*, p. 155.

[32] Barnes, *Tiw*, p. 113 ("*clam* 'A tree-stem thrown over a stream for a bridge' "). See *E.D.D s.v. clam* and *clammer*, a derivative of *clamber*. But the *O.E.D.* gives three other words spelt *clam* which have variants or parallels spelt *clamp*—sb. 1[2], a carpenter's clamp; sb. 2, the edible bivalve; sb. 4, a brick pile ready for firing. We should hesitate therefore to dismiss Hopkins's unsupported form as a mistake.

[33] W. H. Gardner, *Gerard Manley Hopkins*, 1. 109-51 (see esp. pp. 129 ff.). Fr W. A. M. Peters does the same, *Gerard Manley Hopkins*, pp. 64ff.

[34] *Letters*, p. 218.

kins in "That Nature is a Heraclitean Fire", namely "to race or scamper" has been traced no further back than 1830.[35]

A few lines from "The Wreck of the *Deutschland*", st. 19, will provide several examples of his ability to heighten current language—an expression of Hopkins's which has been much misunderstood:

> And the inboard seas run swirling and hawling;
>   The rash smart sloggering brine
> Blinds her. . . .[36]

Here Raymond Schoder observes: " '*Hawling*': not a recognised word; probably intended as equivalent for 'howling'." He adds (with a dash to indicate "an unlikely meaning") "old spelling for *hauling*".[37] Now Hopkins, when he is introducing an unusual word into his verse, most often yokes it with another (here *swirling*) the significance of which it extends and fortifies. The *Oxford English Dictionary* records the form *hawl* as a current variant of *haul*, of which two connotations are specially relevant: "1. to pull or draw with force or violence; to drag, tug (esp. in nautical language) . . . 4. Of the wind: To change direction, shift, veer." How exactly "hawling", then, depicts the swerve and drag of the waves: Hopkins was using the technical language of the sea to poetic effect. *Rash*, as an adjective in nineteenth-century dialect use combined notions of violence, clumsiness, and impetuosity. As a noun, in Scotland, it includes a squall of rain. *Smart* yokes together the normal English value it has in "a smart blow", *i.e.* "hard enough to cause pain", with its provincial application to the weather, "severe, sharp". *Sloggering* is the colloquial term for the action of

[35] *Poems*, p. 105. Contr. W. H. Gardner, *Gerard Manley Hopkins*, I. 130.

[36] *Poems*, p. 57.

[37] Schoder, "Interpretive Glossary", in *Immortal Diamond*, edd. Weyand and Schoder, p. 200.

a prize-fighter raining blows on his opponent: behind it lies the dialect "slog: to strike with great force".[38]

Numerous forms which appear to us today as archaic or poetic came from the daily speech of countrymen, to whom Hopkins clearly delighted to listen. "Throstle"[39] was no literary word to him, but the general word for a song thrush, used throughout the countrysides of Scotland, Ireland, and England. So, too, with *darksome*, and *shipwrack*.[40] *Gear* was so common a word in standard English and in dialect for both implements and "dress" that we do not need to invoke Spenser for its origin:

> And all trades, their gear and tackle and trim.[41]

If Hopkins spoke of the blacksmith who would

> *fettle* for the great grey drayhorse his bright
> and battering sandal!

we may be sure he did not have Capulet's harsh command to Juliet in his mind,[42] but the common workmen who used it as we use "fix"—the roadmenders fettling the tracks, the mower fettling his scythe, the cobbler fettling shoes, or the more specific usages—the smith filing down the rough edges of metal and the ostler grooming his horses.

Another common noun to which Hopkins has given an imaginative and stimulating setting is *delf*, which was used for anything *delved* or dug—a pit, a stone-quarry, a ditch, a coalmine. Looking into the starlit skies Hopkins fancies he sees

> Down in dim woods the diamond delves!
> the elves-eyes![43]

---

[38] Cp. *Daily News*, 1871: "slogging blows".
[39] *Poems*, p. 77.   [40] *Poems*, pp. 89, 61.
[41] *Poems*, p. 69. Contr. W. H. Gardner, *Gerard Manley Hopkins*, I. 130.
[42] *Romeo and Juliet*, III. v. 153.   [43] *Poems*, p. 66.

In "The Windhover" he tried to rescue from the oblivion threatening it the word *selion* or *sillyon* (15th cent. *sellion*) once current in Northumberland and Yorkshire, but in his own day surviving mainly in Lincolnshire as a legal term. It was used of a strip of ploughed land, or as a general term in deeds for a portion of land.[44]

> No wonder of it: sheer plod makes plough down
>   sillion
> Shine, . . .[45]

A Hampshire word which he may have picked up as a boy is compounded into poetry in "The Loss of the *Eurydice*":

> And flockbells off the aerial
>   Downs' forefalls beat to the burial.[46]

Young students forget that *aerial* as a noun dates only from the beginning of our own century, and that *falls* (around the Isle of Wight) referred to steep fields or cliff sides. The ship went down within sound of the sheepbells from the meadow-downs which sloped sharply to the land's edge, almost suspended in air. "Aerial downs" parallels the precipitous feeling of another Hampshire word, *hangers*, which Cobbett in his *Rural Rides* defined as "woods on the sides of very steep hills", such that "the trees and underwood hang, in some sort, to the ground, instead of standing on it."

Two instances, more complicated, may be quoted in support of our plea that the meaning attributed to a strange word should be in full harmony with its context. "The Leaden Echo and Golden Echo" is a chorus resembling Walt Whitman's work in one superficial way (though Hopkins was perturbed at the comparison)[47]—

---

[44] Ogilvie gives it as a local word; the *E.D.D.* quotes Lincolnshire instances from 1851 and 1876.
[45] *Poems*, p. 69.   [46] *Poems*, p. 72.
[47] *Letters*, pp. 154-8; *Poems*, p. 91.

it obtains some of its effects through an array of colourful objects and verbs reduplicating each other in groups, but each selected with infinite care. He joins "ruck and wrinkle" in mutual support. *Ruck* must have entered the language in remote times, since it is related to old Norse *hrukka*. But it survived many hundreds of years before becoming a book word. *Rucked* (in the sense of "having folds") has been found in a manuscript of 1600, but the word did not come into ordinary literary use until well on into the Victorian age. In 1862 Barnes printed it as a dialect word and found it advisable to gloss it fully: "a plait, fold, wrinkle".[48] Hopkins goes on to link "maiden gear" and "gallantry".[49] A crux occurs later:

> O then, weary then whý should we tread? O why
>   are we so haggard at the heart, so care-coiled,
>   care-killed, so fagged, so fashed, so cogged, so
>   cumbered, . . .

The usual interpretation of *cogged* is "deceived, cheated; loaded (of falsified dice)".[50] But such a meaning jars with its context, coming as it does between *fashed* (wearied, vexed) and *cumbered*. Now there is a widespread dialect word *cagged*, meaning "grieved, vexed, annoyed, offended". Its pronunciation in various dialects would approximate closely to *cogged*, with which Hopkins may have confused it.[51] The meaning here seems to me to be as certainly indicated by the companion participles as is a different meaning of *cog* in the Shakespearian context:

> I cannot flatter and speak fair,
> Smile in men's faces, smooth, deceive and cog.[52]

[48] Barnes, *Tiw*, p. 182.

[49] In the sense of jewels, pretty ornaments.

[50] *Immortal Diamond*, edd. Weyand and Schoder, p. 211; cp. W. H. Gardner, in *Poems*, Third Edn, p. 241.

[51] Cp. *fag grass*, which often appears as *fog*, and other examples in E.D.D.

[52] *Richard III*, i. iii. 48.

Another example of assimilation of meanings may possibly have occurred in "That Nature is a Heraclitean Fire" where:

> Delightfully the bright wind boisterous ǀ ropes,
>   wrestles, beats earth bare
> Of yestertempest's creases; ǀ in pool and
>   rutpeel parches
> Squandering ooze to squeezed ǀ dough. . . .[53]

Yestertempest is built by analogy from the numerous dialect compounds: *yester-morning*, *yester-tale* (of something which happened long since), *yester-week*, *yester-evening*. But *ropes* is not immediately intelligible. Hopkins, however, may often have heard lay brothers referring to the harrow having "rope the weeds" in the field. This was the preterite of the dialect *reap* (variously spelt *rape*, *reep*, *rip*, or *ripe*), amongst the meanings of which we find in the *English Dialect Dictionary*: "3. to gather up weeds, etc. under a harrow; to grub up wood, bushes, etc., 4. to gather up dirt by trailing on the ground; to trail in the mud."[54] We may conjecture that *ropes* was in some way coloured by *reaps* in his mind. "*Squandering* ooze" assumes more vividness when we remember the North Country meaning—dispersing, scattering, spreading about.

Other instances of dialect in Hopkins are more easily identified. "Inversnaid" contains several:

> A windpuff bonnet of fáwn-fróth
> Turns and twindles over the broth
> Of a pool so pitchblack, féll-fró wning
> It rounds and rounds Despair to drowning.[55]

Twindle has been ingeniously described by Professor Gardner as "obviously a Carrollian compound of *twist*, *twiddle*, *spindle* and (as eddies do) *dwindle*".[56] But Hop-

[53] *Poems*, p. 105.
[54] Cp. the Chaucerian *ropen*, from *reap*.   [55] *Poems*, p. 89.
[56] W. H. Gardner, *Gerard Manley Hopkins*, I. 117.

kins would also know the Lancashire verb to *twindle*, "to bring forth twins"—here applicable to the breaking up of the foam into two. There is also an old verb *to twind*, meaning "to twist, twine, wind or turn".[57] The next verse of "Inversnaid" has the phrase "Degged with dew" from the northern dialect word to *sprinkle*.[58]

"Ribblesdale", composed during Hopkins's third spell at Stonyhurst in 1882, speaks of the landscape with "leavès throng and louchèd low grass". Doubting whether Dixon would understand it, when Hopkins sent it to him he added:

"louchèd" is a coinage of mine and is to mean much the same as *slouched, slouching*. And I mean "throng" for an adjective as we use it here in Lancashire.[59]

Throng, in its sense "crowded, thick, close set" has become obsolete in standard English, but its dialect use was vigorous in Lancashire, and still occurs in Scots. When we realise that *louch* for *slouch* is also a common dialect word, found in at least six English counties, we can see how the poet's unconscious memory of dialect forms and forces came into play when he was composing.

[57] *O.E.D.*
[58] Barnes, *Tiw*, p. 217, connects with word *dag*, meaning "dew or mist". [59] *Correspondence*, p. 109.

BIBLIOGRAPHY

Where two or more editions are listed, refs.
in the text are to those marked *.

I. WORKS BY HOPKINS

1. Standard Editions

Poems. First Edn., ed. Robert Bridges, London 1918. Second Edn.,
ed. Charles Williams, London 1930. Third Edn., ed. W. H.
Gardner, London 1948; revised, with additional poems, London 1956. *Fourth Edn., edd. W. H. Gardner and N. H.
MacKenzie, London 1967.

The Letters of Gerard Manley Hopkins to Robert Bridges, ed. C. C. Abbott,
London 1935; revised 1955.

The Correspondence of Gerard Manley Hopkins and Richard Watson Dixon,
ed. C. C. Abbott, London 1935; revised 1955.

*Further Letters of Gerard Manley Hopkins, including his Correspondence with
Coventry Patmore*, ed. C. C. Abbott, London 1938; *2nd edn.,
revised and enlarged, London 1956.

The Note-books and Papers, ed. Humphry House, London 1936.

The Journals and Papers, ed. Humphry House, completed by Graham
Storey, London 1959.

The Sermons and Devotional Writings, ed. Christopher Devlin, *S.J.*,
London 1959.

2. Selections

Selected Poems, ed. James Reeves, London 1953.

A Hopkins Reader, ed. John Pick, London 1953. Contains selections
from his poems (without annotations), letters, sermons, etc.

Poems and Prose, ed. W. H. Gardner, Penguin Poets, Harmondsworth,
London 1953; revised 1963, etc.

Hopkins Selections, ed. Graham Storey, New Oxford English Series,
London (O.U.P.) 1967.

II. WORKS BY OTHERS

AUDEN, W. H. "The Knight of the Infinite", in *The New Republic*,
III (1944), pp. 223 ff.

BAUM, PAULL F. "Sprung Rhythm", in *PMLA*, LXXIV (1959),
pp. 418-25.

BENDER, TODD K. *Gerard Manley Hopkins: The Classical Background and Critical Reception of his Work*, Baltimore 1966.

BISCHOFF (s.j.), D. A. "The Manuscripts of Hopkins", in *Thought*, XXVI (1951-2), pp. 551-80.

BLISS (s.j.), GEOFFREY. "In a Poet's Workshop", in *The Month*, CLXVII (1936), pp. 160-7, 525-35.

BONN (s.j.), J. L. "Greco-Roman Verse Theory and Gerard Manley Hopkins", in *Immortal Diamond*, edd. Weyand and Schoder, pp. 73-92.

BOYLE (s.j.), ROBERT. *Metaphor in Hopkins*, Chapel Hill 1961.

CHARNEY, MAURICE. "A Bibliographical study of Hopkins Criticism, 1918-1949", in *Thought*, XXV (1950), pp. 297-326.

COHEN, SELMA J. "The Poetic Theory of Gerard Manley Hopkins", in *The Philological Quarterly*, XXVI (1947), pp. 1-20.

CREHAN (s.j.), J. H. "More Light on Gerard Hopkins", in *The Month*, n.s., x (1953), pp. 205-14.

DAVIE, DONALD. "Hopkins as a Decadent Critic", in *Purity of Diction in English Verse*, London 1952, pp. 160-82.

DEVLIN (s.j.), CHRISTOPHER. "The Image and the Word", in *The Month*, n.s., III (1950), pp. 114-27, 191-202.

DOWNES, DAVID. *Gerard Manley Hopkins: A Study of his Ignatian Spirit*, London 1959.

GARDNER, W. H. "The Wreck of the *Deutschland*", in *Essays and Studies*, XXI (1935), pp. 124-52.

——. *Gerard Manley Hopkins: A Study of Poetic Idiosyncrasy in Relation to Poetic Tradition*, 2 vols., London 1944, 1949; 2nd edn., 1962.

GHISELIN, BREWSTER. "Reading Sprung Rhythms", in *Poetry*, LXX (1947), pp. 86-93.

GRAVES, WILLIAM L. "Gerard Manley Hopkins as Composer", in *Victorian Poetry*, I (1963), pp. 146-55.

GRIGSON, GEOFFREY. *Gerard Manley Hopkins*, Writers and their Work, London 1955.

GROSS, HARVEY. *Sound and Form in Modern Poetry*, Ann Arbor 1964.

HARTMAN, G. T. *The Unmediated Vision*, New Haven 1954.

HEUSER, ALAN. *The Shaping Vision of Gerard Manley Hopkins*, London 1958.

HOLLOWAY, SISTER MARCELLA M. *The Prosodic Theory of Gerard Manley Hopkins*, Washington, D.C. 1947.

HOUSE, HUMPHRY, *All in Due Time*, London 1955.

IYENGAR, K. R. S. *Gerard Manley Hopkins: The Man and the Poet*, London 1948.

KEATING, JOHN E. *The Wreck of the Deutschland: An Essay and Commentary*, Kent (Ohio) 1963.

KENYON CRITICS, THE. *Gerard Manley Hopkins*, New York 1945.

LAHEY (s.j.), G. F. *Gerard Manley Hopkins*, London 1930.

LEAVIS, F. R. *New Bearings in English Poetry*, London 1932.

——. "The Letters of Gerard Manley Hopkins", in *Scrutiny*, IV (1935), pp. 216-31; reprinted in *The Common Pursuit*, London 1952.

——. "Gerard Manley Hopkins", in *Scrutiny* XII (1944), pp. 82-93; reprinted in *The Common Pursuit*, London 1952.

LEES, FRANCIS N. *Gerard Manley Hopkins*, Columbia Essays on Modern Writers, New York and London 1966.

LILLY, GWENETH. "The Welsh Influence in the Poetry of Gerard Manley Hopkins", in *The Modern Language Review*, XXXVIII (1943), pp. 192-205.

MACCOLL, D. S. "Patmore and Hopkins—Sense and Nonsense in English Prosody", in *The London Mercury* XXXVIII (1938), pp. 217-24.

MACKENZIE, NORMAN H. "Hopkins among the Victorians— Form in Art and Nature", in *English Studies Today*, 3rd ser., ed. G. I. Duthie, Edinburgh 1964.

——. "Hopkins MSS—Old Losses and New Finds", in *T.L.S.*, 18 Mar. 1965, p. 220.

——. "Gerard and Grace Hopkins: Some new Links", in *The Month*, n.s., XXXIII (1965), pp. 347 ff.

MELLOWN, E. W. "Gerard Manley Hopkins and his Public, 1889-1918", in *Modern Philology*, LVII (1959), pp. 94 ff.

——. "The Reception of Gerard Manley Hopkins' *Poems*, 1918-30", in *Modern Philology*, LXIII (1965), pp. 38-51.

MILES, JOSEPHINE. "The Sweet and Lovely Language", in the Kenyon Critics vol., ch. 4, 1945.

MORRIS, DAVID. *The Poetry of Gerard Manley Hopkins and T. S. Eliot in the Light of the Donne Tradition*, Berne 1953.

OCHSHORN, MYRON G. "Hopkins the Critic", in *Yale Review*, LIV (1965), pp. 346-67.

ONG (S.J.), WALTER. "Sprung Rhythm and the Life of English Poetry", in *Immortal Diamond*, edd. Weyand and Schoder.

PETERS (S.J.), W. A. M. *Gerard Manley Hopkins: A Critical Essay towards the Understanding of his Poetry*, London 1948.

PHARE, ELIZABETH. *The Poetry of Gerard Manley Hopkins*, Cambridge 1933.

PICK, JOHN. *Gerard Manley Hopkins: Priest and Poet*, London 1942.

——. "Gerard Manley Hopkins", in *The Victorian Poets: A Guide to Research*, ed. F. E. Faverty, Cambridge (Mass.) 1956.

READ, HERBERT. "The Poetry of Gerard Manley Hopkins", in *English Critical Essays, 20th Century*, ed. Phyllis M. Jones, London 1933.

RICHARDS, I. A. "Gerard Hopkins", in *Dial*, No. 131 (1926), pp. 195-203.

——. *Practical Criticism*, London 1929, pp. 80-90.

RITZ, JEAN-GEORGES, *Robert Bridges and Gerard Hopkins, 1863-1889: A Literary Friendship*, London 1960.

——. *Le Poète Gérard Manley Hopkins, S.J.: L'homme et l'œuvre*, Paris 1963.

RUGGLES, ELEANOR. *Gerard Manley Hopkins: A Life*, London 1947.

SCHNEIDER, ELISABETH. "Sprung Rhythm: A Chapter in the Evolution of Nineteenth Century Verse", *PMLA*, LXXX (1965), pp. 237-53.

——. "The Wreck of the *Deutschland*: A New Reading", *PMLA*, LXXXI (1966), pp. 110-22.

SCHODER (S.J.), RAYMOND. "An Interpretive Glossary of Difficult Words in the Poems", in *Immortal Diamond*, edd. Weyand and Schoder.

——. See WEYAND, NORMAN.

SHEA (S.J.), F. X. "Another Look at 'The Windhover' ", in *Victorian Poetry*, II (1964), pp. 219-39.

STOBIE, MARGARET R. "Patmore's Theory and Hopkins' Practice", in *University of Toronto Quarterly*, XIX (1949), pp. 60-80.

STOREY, GRAHAM. "Six New Letters of Gerard Manley Hopkins", in *The Month*, n.s., XIX (1958), pp. 263-70.

THOMAS (S.J.), ALFRED, "G. M. Hopkins and The Silver Jubilee Album", in *The Library*, 5th ser., XX (1965), pp. 148-52.

TILLEMANS, T. "Is Hopkins a Modern Poet?", in *English Studies*, XXIV (1942), pp. 90-5.

TRENEER, ANNE. "The Criticism of Gerard Manley Hopkins", in *Penguin New Writing*, ed. J. Lehmann, No. 40 (1950), pp. 98-115.

WEYAND (S.J.), NORMAN, and R. V. SCHODER (S.J.), (edd.). *Immortal Diamond: Studies in Gerard Manley Hopkins*, London and New York 1949.

WARREN, AUSTIN. "Instress of Inscape", in the Kenyon Critics volume, 1945.

WHITEHALL, HAROLD. "Sprung Rhythm", in the Kenyon Critics volume, 1945.

WINTERS, YVOR. "The Poetry of Gerard Manley Hopkins", in *Hudson Review*, 1949; reprinted in *The Function of Criticism*, Denver 1957.

——. "The Audible Reading of Poetry", in *Hudson Review* (1951); reprinted in *The Function of Criticism*.